and  er

UNIVERSITY OF NOTRE DAME
STUDIES IN THE
PHILOSOPHY OF RELIGION

Number 1

Rationality
and Religious Belief

Edited with an Introduction by
C. F. DELANEY

UNIVERSITY OF NOTRE DAME PRESS
NOTRE DAME   LONDON

Copyright © 1979 by
University of Notre Dame Press
Notre Dame, Indiana 46556

9 8 7 6 5 4 3 2 1

Library of Congress Cataloging in Publication Data

Main entry under title:

Rationality and religious belief.

(Notre Dame studies in the philosophy of religion;
no. 1)
    Includes bibliographical references.
    1. Religion—Philosophy—Addresses, essays, lectures.
I. Delaney, Cornelius, F. II. Series.
BL51.R29   200'.1   79-63359
ISBN 0-268-01602-X
ISBN 0-268-01603-8 pbk.

Manufactured in the United States of America

Contents

Contributors

ROBERT M. ADAMS is Professor of Philosophy and Chairman of the Philosophy Department at UCLA. He has written extensively in professional journals on philosophy of religion, on ethics, and on the interface of the two.

G. E. M. ANSCOMBE is Professor of Philosophy at Cambridge University. She is the author of *Intention, Three Philosophers* (with P. Geach), *Introduction to Wittgenstein's Tractatus,* and numerous professional articles in philosophy of mind and ethics.

DAVID BURRELL is Professor of Philosophy and Chairman of the Theology Department at the University of Notre Dame. He is the author of *Analogy and Philosophical Language, Exercises in Religious Understanding, Aquinas: God and Action,* and numerous articles in philosophy of religion and theology.

FREDERICK CROSSON is Professor of Philosophy and director of the "Center for Philosophy of Religion" at the University of Notre Dame. He is co-editor of *The Modeling of Mind, Philosophy and Cybernetics* and *Science and Contemporary Society* and the author of articles in philosophy of religion, political philosophy, and phenomenology.

C. F. DELANEY is Professor of Philosophy and Chairman of the Philosophy Department at the University of Notre Dame. He is the author of *Mind and Nature,* co-author of *The Synoptic Vision: Essays on the Philosophy of Wilfrid Sellars,* and has published many articles on American philosophy and epistemology.

LANGDON GILKEY is a Professor at the University of Chicago Divinity School. He is the author of *Maker of Heaven and Earth, Religion and the Scientific Future, The Renewal of God Language,* and *The Social and Intellectual Sources of Contemporary Protestant Theology.*

GEORGE MAVRODES is Professor of Philosophy at the University of Michigan. He is the author of *Belief in God: A Study in the Epistemology of Religion,* co-author of *Problems and Perspectives in the Philosophy of Religion,* and editor of *The Rationality of Belief in God.* He has also published articles on the epistemology of religion and on religious language.

ALVIN PLANTINGA is Professor of Philosophy at Calvin College and Adjunct Professor at the University of Notre Dame. He is the author of *God and Other Minds; The Nature of Necessity; God, Freedom and Evil;* and numerous professional papers in the areas of metaphysics and the philosophy of religion.

JOHN SMITH is Professor of Philosophy at Yale University and the author of numerous books on both American philosophy and philosophy of religion. Among the latter are his *Reason and God, Experience and God, Religion and Empiricism,* and *The Analogy of Experience.*

Introduction

When the issue of the rationality of religious belief is raised, very often the meaning of 'rationality' is assumed to be fixed and unproblematic and suitable as it stands as a measuring rod vis-à-vis religious belief. The papers in this volume call this simplistic strategy into question. Together they exhibit the fact that our specific question about the rationality of religious belief should be seen to be as much about rationality as about religion, while also exhibiting the fact that this question should address religion concretely as a human practice rather than abstractly as a system of propositions. Obviously, each paper comes at this general question from a different angle and not all the issues come up in each paper, but it is our hope that together they open up new perspectives on this matter and will thereby contribute fruitfully to on-going discussions in the philosophy of religion.

While the individual studies in this volume are intended as self-intelligible units, there is a certain order to the whole which could be profitably borne in mind. The papers of Plantinga and Mavrodes examine the question of rationality directly and somewhat abstractly, whereas those of Smith and Gilkey situate our discussion of the rationality of religion in the dialectic of the history of thought. The papers of Burrell and Adams come at the question through the technical notion of "proof," while those of Anscombe and Crosson focus on the notion of "belief" as it is concretely situated either in ordinary language or in the classic documents of the Christian tradition. It is our hope that these papers in a mutually supportive way illumine some of the many facets of the question at issue.

Alvin Plantinga's paper "Is Belief in God Rational?" meets the issue head-on. He sees the easy strategy of simply measuring this specific belief by the definition of rationality blocked by the unavailability of any acceptable definition of rationality. We don't seem to have a satisfactory set of necessary and sufficient conditions for rational belief, nor is clarification achieved when we back off to the notion of "sufficient evidence." Bracketing these deep questions, Plantinga then explores a foundational picture of knowledge whereby a belief is rational if and only if it is evident with respect to those propositions that constitute the foundation of a person's noetic structure. The crucial questions here turn out to be about the conditions a belief has to meet to be in the foundations of one's noetic structure. Self-evidence, incorrigibility, immediacy, and evident-to-the-senses are the criteria examined prior to raising the question: why shouldn't belief in God be among the foundations of my noetic structure? Upon raising this question, Plantinga finds no reason at all why the theist's belief in God cannot be in the foundations of a rational noetic structure. If the criteria of admission to the foundations are tightened so as to exclude belief in God, they also exclude many propositions the foundationalist wants included, and if they are loosened so as to admit these latter propositions, there seems to be no reason to exclude belief in God. Accordingly, Plantinga concludes that on this model of knowledge there is nothing contrary to reason about taking belief in God as basic and hence as rational.

In "Rationality and Religious Belief—A Perverse Question" George Mavrodes distinguishes between rationality-oriented approaches to this question and truth-oriented approaches and then explores some possible combinations of truth value and rationality. The cases where truth and rationality go together and where falsehood and irrationality are paired are unproblematic. But what about the "perverse" situations wherein truth and irrationality go together or where falsehood and rationality are paired? After exploring some ways of blocking these perverse combinations in our noetic structure, Mavrodes makes it clear that if forced to choose between the two, he would go with the claims of truth over those of rationality.

John Smith's "Faith, Belief, and the Problem of Rationality in Religion" situates the discussion of our question in the history of philosophy. After identifying other polarities relevant to our topic, Smith focuses on the polarity between secular rationality and religious tradition. The standard of rationality is seen to be the crux of the problem, and a sharp contrast is drawn between the ontological standard of someone like Anselm, which allows for the rationality of religion, and the scientific standard of someone like Wittgenstein, which results in religion's being viewed as irrational. Smith insists that setting this standard is a philosophical task and argues for a recovery of constructive philosophy with its ontological dimension as a medium for understanding and interpreting religious belief. He does not, however, advocate a simple return to past modes of thought but rather the imaginative construction of a new dynamic experiential metaphysic that will enable us to attain an understanding of faith under contemporary conditions.

In "The Dialectic of Christian Belief: Rational, Incredible, Credible," Langdon Gilkey attempts to uncover a basic dialectic in the relation of rationality to Christian belief, a dialectic that moves from rationality through incredibility to credibility. This thesis is illustrated through the relation of Christianity to historicity. The structure of our historical being gives rise to the claim that temporal finitude has need of a divine creative ground (rationality), yet the character of our concrete historical existence as estranged and alienated continually obscures that divine ground through meaninglessness and despair (incredibility). Finally, and paradoxically, it is in our relation of estrangement from the divine as ground that the divine manifests itself as redemptive and therein is found the fullness of faith (credibility). Moreover, these moments in that total system of symbols which is Christianity are so interrelated that the rationality of the first and the credibility of the third degenerate into incredibility if either element is separated from the other. The total system of Christian symbols is seen to be neither rational nor irrational but to be credible as a valid symbolic thematization and description of the totality of our concrete experience.

David Burrell's "Religious Belief and Rationality" re-examines, both historically and philosophically, the classic notion of "proof" as it functions in the justification of religious belief. It is his contention that the classical proofs are not intended as demonstrations, nor do they function as the founda-tions of a belief in God; rather, they play a role in "predis-posing" one to religious belief and offer a kind of retro-spective justification from within the belief context. He argues his thesis with regard to Anselm, Aquinas, Augustine, and Kant by situating them all in the "faith seeking understanding" tradition. Burrell develops a notion of pragmatic presuppo-sition in showing that the practices ingredient in rational inquiry presuppose an operative belief in an overarching unity and that the practices of religious faith presuppose a living connection with a divine reality. He then suggests that it is reasonable to identify the presuppositions of each practice and thus construct a path from reason to faith. Burrell points out, however, that to the degree that this provides a justifica-tion for religious belief, the justification is retrospective rather than prospective and, furthermore, that this internal kind of justification is the only kind appropriate to the religious enterprise.

The issue of proof is explored still further in Robert Adams' "Moral Arguments for Theistic Belief," but he shifts the focus from the cosmological to the moral arguments. First, Adams explores the argument from the nature of right and wrong. Here he refines and defends the divine command theory of ethics, specifying its advantages over other meta-ethical views and responding to some of the standard objections to it. This theory, of course, entails the existence of God. Secondly, Adams examines moral arguments for the existence of God which are Kantian in structure. He distinguishes between theoretical (arguments having an ethical premise purporting to prove the truth or probability of theism) and practical (arguments purporting to give ethical or other practical reasons for be-lieving that God exists) moral arguments, and then discusses in some detail the legitimacy of practical moral arguments. Thirdly, he explores an argument common to both classical and Kantian theism that focuses on the harmony of true self-interest with morality, the coincidence of happiness and virtue. Adams concludes with a discussion of moral arguments, not for God's existence, but for God's goodness—arguments to the effect that "if there is a God, he is morally very good."

Elizabeth Anscombe's "What Is It to Believe Someone?" prepares the ground for a discussion of religious faith by exploring the notions of belief and testimony as they function in familiar contexts. She is interested in the concept of 'believing God' as in "Abraham believed God" and approaches the notion through the expression "believing x (person) that p." She notes that this notion of testimony is not only important for theology and philosophy of religion but is also crucial for epistemology. Testimony is the source of most of our knowledge. After considering cases of believing people who are perceived, Anscombe moves to a discussion of communication where the speaker is not perceived. After specifying certain further beliefs that are involved in believing someone, she concludes by raising the problematic case wherein I believe what someone tells me only because I believe he is both a liar and misinformed. This raises the question of truthfulness and rightness in this whole matter of testimony.

In the final piece, Frederick Crosson's "Religion and Faith in St. Augustine's Confessions," the overriding question of the whole volume is approached through one of the classic documents in the Christian tradition. After distinguishing between three general modes of comprehending our world, i.e., myths, histories, and conceptual accounts, Crosson maintains that the conceptual enterprise which is the philosophy of religion must take its beginning from the more symbolic things people say and do when they are relating themselves to what is holy. Philosophical understanding should at least have its origin from within that concrete form of life which is religion. Crosson illustrates this point through an analysis of Augustine's *Confessions*. Augustine is portrayed as never sacrificing reason while always remaining sensitive to the fact that religion tells stories to express its fundamental beliefs and that it is these stories themselves which bear and retain the primary and distinctive level of religious meaning. Hence, our quest for rationality in religion, if it is not to be Procrustean, should focus not on certain isolated propositions abstractly analyzed but on how certain stories and histories express and embody a belief system.

Given these brief summaries, then, it should be reasonably clear how the themes of "being critical about rationality itself" and "being concrete about religion" weave their way through the various discussions of rationality and religious belief collected in this volume. The simplistic strategy of characterizing religion via some abstract set of propositions and then judging it by means of an independently determined standard of rationality has been called into question from several perspectives. Religion is seen to be more than a set of beliefs, and even belief itself is seen to involve more than mere assent to abstract propositions. Concretely, religion is encountered as a complex set of practices bearing on the relation of man to what is holy, practices which are intricately interrelated with all those other practices the sum of which define human existence. Nor are the criteria of rationality eternally fixed and simply given to us for unquestioned use as measuring rods. Rationality too has its history, and the practice of selecting the standards of one domain as the model of rationality *uberhaupt* has, in more than one instance, resulted in an impoverished comprehension of the domain not only of religion but of ethics, history, mathematics, and even experimental science. Religion is not an abstraction, nor is rationality a genus. Moreover, our two themes of "being critical about rationality" and "being concrete about religion" can be seen to be related inasmuch as often it is the very abstractness of our philosophical accounts that leads to an impoverished grasp of religion as well as an idealized picture of rationality. It may well be that only in a continual reversion to the concrete realm of historical practice can an understanding of either religion or epistemology be achieved.

C. F. DELANEY

Is Belief in God Rational?

ALVIN PLANTINGA

What I mean to discuss, in this paper, is the question its title formulates. That is to say, I wish to discuss the question "Is it rational, or reasonable, or rationally acceptable, to believe in God?" I mean to *discuss* this question, not answer it. My initial aim is not to argue that religious belief *is* rational (although I think it is) but to try to understand this question.

The first thing to note is that I have stated the question misleadingly. What I really want to discuss is whether it is rational to believe that God exists—that there is such a person as God. Of course there is an important difference between believing that God exists and believing *in* God. To believe that God exists is just to accept a certain proposition—the proposition that there really is such a person as God—as true. According to the book of James (2:19) the devils believe this proposition, and they tremble. To believe *in* God, however, is to trust him, to commit your life to him, to make his purposes your own. The devils do not do that. So there is a difference between believing in God and believing that he exists; for purposes of economy, however, I shall use the phrase 'belief in God' as a synonym for 'belief that God exists'.

Our question, therefore, is whether belief in God is rational. This question is widely asked and widely answered. Many philosophers—most prominently, those in the great tradition of natural theology—have argued that belief in God *is* rational; they have typically done so by providing what they took to be *demonstrations* or *proofs* of God's existence. Many others have argued that belief in God is *ir*rational. If we call those

7

of the first group 'natural theologians', perhaps we should call those of the second 'natural atheologians'. (That would at any rate be kinder than calling them 'unnatural theologians'.) J. L. Mackie, for example, opens his statement of the problem of evil as follows: "I think, however, that a more telling criticism can be made by way of the traditional problem of evil. Here it can be shown, not merely that religious beliefs lack rational support, but that they are positively irrational. . . ."[1] And a very large number of philosophers take it that a central question—perhaps *the* central question—of philosophy of religion is the question whether religious belief in general and belief in God in particular is rationally acceptable.[2]

Now an apparently straightforward and promising way to approach this question would be to take a definition of rationality and see whether belief in God conforms to it. The chief difficulty with this appealing course, however, is that no such definition of rationality seems to be available. If there *were* such a definition, it would set out some conditions for a belief's being rationally acceptable—conditions that are severally necessary and jointly sufficient. That is, each of the conditions would have to be met by a belief that is rationally acceptable; and if a belief met all the conditions, then it would follow that it is rationally acceptable. But it is monumentally difficult to find any non-trivial necessary conditions at all. Surely, for example, we cannot insist that S's belief that p is rational only if it is *true*. For consider Newton's belief that if x, y and z are moving colinearly, then the motion of z with respect to x is the sum of the motions of y with respect to x and z with respect to y. No doubt Newton was rational in accepting this belief; yet it was false, at least if contemporary physicists are to be trusted. And if they aren't—that is, if they are wrong in contradicting Newton—then *they* exemplify what I'm speaking of; they rationally believe a proposition which, as it turns out, is false.

Nor can we say that a belief is rationally acceptable only if it is possibly true, not necessarily false in the broadly logical sense.[3] For example, I might do the sum $735 + 421 + 9,216$ several times and get the same answer: $10,362$. I am then rational in believing that 735 + 421 + 9,216 = 10,362, even though the fact is I've made the same error each time—failed to carry a '1' from the first column—and thus believe what is necessarily false. Or I might be a mathematical neophyte who hears from his teacher that every continuous function is differentiable. I need not be irrational in believing this, despite the fact that it is necessarily false. Examples of this sort can be multiplied.

So this question presents something of an initial enigma in that it is by no means easy to say what it is for a belief to be rational. And the fact is those philosophers who ask this question about belief in God do not typically try to answer it by giving necessary and sufficient conditions for rational belief. Instead, they typically ask whether the believer has *evidence* or *sufficient evidence* for his belief; or they may try to argue that in fact there is sufficient evidence for the proposition that there is *no* God; but in any case they try to answer this question by finding evidence for or against theistic belief. Philosophers who think there are sound arguments for the existence of God—the natural theologians—claim there is good evidence *for* this proposition; philosophers who believe that there are sound arguments for the non-existence of God naturally claim that there is evidence *against* this proposition. But they concur in holding that belief in God is rational only if there is, on balance, a preponderance of evidence for it— or less radically, only if there is not, on balance, a preponderance of evidence against it.

The nineteenth-century philosopher W. K. Clifford provides a splendid if somewhat strident example of the view that the believer in God must have evidence if he is not to be irrational. Here he does not discriminate against religious belief; he apparently holds that a belief of any sort at all is rationally acceptable only if there is sufficient evidence for it. And he goes on to insist that it is wicked, immoral, monstrous, and perhaps even impolite to accept a belief for which one does not have sufficient evidence:

> Whoso would deserve well of his fellows in this matter will guard the purity of his belief with a very fanaticism of jealous care, lest at any time it should rest on an unworthy object, and catch a stain which can never be wiped away.

He adds that if a

> belief has been accepted on insufficient evidence, the pleasure is
> a stolen one. Not only does it deceive ourselves by giving us a
> sense of power which we do not really possess, but it is sinful,
> because it is stolen in defiance of our duty to mankind. That duty
> is to guard ourselves from such beliefs as from a pestilence which
> may shortly master our body and spread to the rest of the town.

And finally:

> To sum up: it is wrong always, everywhere, and for anyone to
> believe anything upon insufficient evidence.[4]

(It is not hard to detect, in these quotations, the "tone of
robustious pathos" with which William James credits him.)
Clifford finds it utterly obvious, furthermore, that those who
believe in God do indeed so believe on insufficient evidence
and thus deserve the above abuse. A believer in God is, on his
view, at best a harmless pest and at worst a menace to society;
in either case he should be discouraged.

Now there are some initial problems with Clifford's claim.
For example, he doesn't tell us how *much* evidence is sufficient.
More important, the notion of evidence is about as difficult
as that of rationality: What is evidence? How do you know
when you have some? How do you know when you have sufficient or enough? Suppose, furthermore, that a person thinks
he has sufficient evidence for a proposition p when in fact
he does not—would he then be irrational in believing p?
Presumably a person can have sufficient evidence for what is
false—else either Newton did not have sufficient evidence for
his physical beliefs or contemporary physicists don't have
enough for *theirs*. Suppose, then, that a person has sufficient
evidence for the false proposition that he has sufficient evidence
for p. Is he then irrational in believing p? Presumably not;
but if not, having sufficient evidence is not, contrary to
Clifford's claim, a necessary condition for believing p
rationally.

But suppose we temporarily concede that these initial difficulties can be resolved and take a deeper look at Clifford's

position. What is essential to it is the claim that we must evaluate the rationality of belief in God by examining its relation to *other* propositions. We are directed to estimate its rationality by determining whether we have *evidence* for it—whether we know, or at any rate rationally believe, some other propositions which stand in the appropriate relation to the proposition in question. And belief in God is rational, or reasonable, or rationally acceptable, on this view, only if there are other propositions with respect to which it is thus evident.

According to the Cliffordian position, then, there is a set of propositions E such that my belief in God is rational if and only if it is evident with respect to E—if and only if E constitutes, on balance, evidence for it. But what propositions are to be found in E? Do we know that belief in God is not itself in E? If it *is*, of course, then it is certainly evident with respect to E. How does a proposition get into E anyway? How do we decide which propositions are the ones such that my belief in God is rational if and only if it is evident with respect to them? Should we say that E contains the propositions that I *know*? But then, for our question to be interesting, we should first have to argue or agree that I don't know that God exists —that I only *believe* it, whether rationally or irrationally. This position is widely taken for granted, and indeed taken for granted by theists as well as others. But why should the latter concede that he doesn't know that God exists—that at best he rationally believes it? The Bible regularly speaks of *knowledge* in this context—not just rational or well-founded belief. Of course it is true that the believer has *faith*—faith in God, faith in what He reveals, faith that God exists—but this by no means settles the issue. The question is whether he doesn't also *know* that God exists. Indeed, according to the Heidelberg Catechism, knowledge is an essential element of faith, so that one has true faith that *p* only if he knows that *p:*

> True faith is not only a certain (i.e., sure) knowledge whereby I hold for truth all that God has revealed in His word, but also a deep-rooted assurance created in me by the Holy Spirit through the gospel that not only others but I too have had my sins forgiven, have been made forever right with God and have been granted salvation. (Q 21)

So from this point of view a man has true faith that p only if he knows that p, and also meets a certain further condition: roughly (where p is a universal proposition) that of accepting the universal instantiation of p with respect to himself. Now of course the theist may be unwilling to concede that he does not have true faith that God exists; accordingly he may be unwilling to concede—initially, at any rate—that he does not know, but only believes that God exists.

How, then, do I determine whether I *do* know, as opposed to merely believe, that God exists? A typical traditional suggestion is that you know what you truly believe and have adequate evidence for—that is, you know that p if and only if you believe p, p is true, and you have adequate or sufficient evidence for p. But then to discover whether I know that God exists I must discover whether I believe it, whether it is true, and whether I have adequate evidence for it. This last, of course—the question whether I have adequate evidence for my belief in God—reintroduces the very questions we have been examining. The present suggestion, therefore, is unhelpful; we are still left with our query: Why shouldn't I take E as including the proposition that God exists, thus producing an easy answer to the question whether my belief in God is rational?

Now of course the Cliffordian will not be at all eager to agree that belief in God belongs in E. But why not? To answer we must take a deeper look at his position. Suppose we say that the assemblage of beliefs a person holds, together with the various logical and epistemic relations that hold among them, constitutes that person's *noetic structure*. Now what the Cliffordian really holds is that for each person S there is a set F of beliefs such that a proposition p is rational or rationally acceptable for S only if p is evident with respect to F—only if, that is, the propositions in F constitute, on balance, evidence for p. Let us say that this set F of propositions is the *foundation of S's noetic structure*. On this view every noetic structure has a foundation; and a proposition is rational for S, or known by S, or certain for S, only if it stands in the appropriate relation to the foundation of S's noetic structure.

Suppose we call this view *foundationalism*. It is by no means peculiar to Clifford; foundationalism has had a long and distinguished career in the history of philosophy, including among its adherents Plato, Aristotle, Aquinas, Descartes, Leibniz, Locke, and, to leap to the present, Professor Roderick Chisholm. And from the foundationalist point of view, our question must be restated: Is belief in God evident with respect to the foundations of my noetic structure? Clifford, as I say, takes it to be obvious that the answer is *no*. But *is* this obvious? To restate my earlier question: Might it not be that my belief in God is itself in the foundations of my noetic structure? Perhaps it is a member of F, in which case, of course, it will automatically be evident with respect to F.

Here the Cliffordian foundationalist goes further. Not just *any* belief can properly be in the foundations of a person's noetic structure; to be in F a belief must meet some fairly specific conditions. It must be capable of functioning foundationally; it must be capable of bearing its share of the weight of the entire noetic structure. The propositions in F, of course, are not inferred from other propositions and are not accepted on the basis of other propositions. I know the propositions in the foundations of my noetic structure, but not by virtue of knowing *other* propositions; for these are the ones I start with. And so the question the foundationalist asks about belief in God—namely, what is the evidence for it?—is not properly asked about the members of F; these items don't require to be evident with respect to *other* propositions in order to be rationally believed. Accordingly, says the foundationalist, not just any proposition is capable of functioning foundationally; to be so capable, with respect to a person S, a proposition must not need the evidential support of other propositions; it must be such that it is possible that S know *p* but have no evidence for *p*.

Well, suppose all this is so; what kind of propositions *can* function foundationally? Here, of course, different foundationalists give different answers. Aristotle and Aquinas, for example, held that *self-evident* propositions—ones like *all black dogs are black*—belong in the foundations. Aquinas, at least, seems also to hold that propositions "evident to the senses," as he puts it—propositions like *some things change* —belong there. For he believed, of course, that the existence of God is demonstrable; and by this I think he meant that God's existence can be deduced from foundational propositions. He holds, furthermore, that God's existence can be demonstrated "from his effects"—from sensible objects; and in each of the five ways there is a premise that, says Aquinas, is "evident to the senses." I therefore believe Aquinas meant to include such propositions among the foundations. You may think it strange, incidentally, to count Aquinas among the Cliffordians. On this point, however, he probably belongs with them; he held that belief in God is rational only if evident with respect to the foundations. Of course he differs from Clifford in holding that in fact God's existence *is* evident with respect to them; he thinks it follows from members of F by argument forms that are themselves in F. This, indeed, is the burden of his five ways.

According to Aquinas, therefore, self-evident propositions and those evident to the senses belong in the foundations. And when he speaks of propositions of the latter sort, he means such propositions as

    (1) there's a tree over there,

    (2) there is an ash tray on my desk,

    (3) that tree's leaves have turned yellow,

and

    (4) this fender has rusted through.

Other foundationalists—Descartes, for example—argue that what goes into the foundations, in addition to self-evident propositions, are not propositions that, like (1)–(4), entail the existence of such material objects as ashtrays, trees, leaves, and fenders, but more cautious claims; for example:

    (5) I seem to see a red book,

    (6) it seems to me that I see a book with a red cover,

    (7) I seem to see something red,

or even, as Professor Chisholm put its,

> (8) I am appeared redly to.[5]

The foundationalist who opts for propositions like (5)–(8) rather than (1)–(4) has a *prima facie* plausible reason for doing so: Belief in a proposition of the latter sort seems to have a sort of immunity from error not enjoyed by belief in one of the former. I may believe that there is a red ashtray on my desk, or that I see a red ashtray on my desk, when the fact is there is no red ashtray there at all: I am color-blind, or hallucinating, or the victim of an illusion of some sort or other. But it is at the least very much harder to see that I could be wrong in believing that I *seem* to see a red ashtray on my desk—that, in Chisholm's language, I am appeared redly (or red-ashtrayly) to. There are plenty of possible worlds in which I mistakenly believe that there is a red book on my desk; it is at least plausible to hold that there are no possible worlds in which I mistakenly believe that I seem to see a red book there. And this immunity from error may plausibly be taken to provide a reason for distinguishing between propositions like (5)–(8) and (1)–(4), admitting the former but not the latter to the foundations.

There is a small problem here, however: Every necessarily true proposition—every proposition true in all possible worlds—is such that there is no possible world in which I mistakenly believe it. Yet presumably the foundationalist will not be inclined to hold that every necessary proposition I believe is in the foundations of my noetic structure. Consider, for example, Goldbach's Conjecture that every even number greater than two is the sum of two primes. This proposition is either necessarily true or necessarily false, although it isn't presently known which. Suppose it is in fact true, and I believe it, but not because I have found a proof of it; I simply believe it. The foundationalist will presumably hold, in this case, that my belief in Goldbach's Conjecture is necessarily true but not a good candidate for the foundations. Here I truly believe but do not know the proposition in question; so it does not belong among the foundations, and this despite the fact that there is no possible world in which I mistakenly believe it.

Presumably, then, the Cliffordian will not hold that just any necessarily true belief is automatically among the founda tions. He may argue instead that what characterizes propositions like (5)–(8) is not just that it is not possible to believe them mistakenly, but that it is not possible to be mistaken about them. That is to say, a proposition of this sort is like a necessary proposition in that it is not possible for me to believe it mistakenly; it is unlike a necessary proposition, however, in that it is also not possible for me to believe its *denial* mistakenly. If I believe that I am appeared to redly, then it follows that I *am* appeared to redly; but if I believe that I am not appeared to redly, it follows equally that I am not thus appeared to. We might say that propositions meeting this condition are *incorrigible* for me; perhaps we can explain this notion thus:

> (9) p is incorrigible for S at t iff there is no possible world in which S mistakenly believes p at t and no possible world in which S mistakenly believes not-p at t.[6]

According to our paradigm Cliffordian, then, a belief is properly in the foundations of my noetic structure only if it is either self-evident or incorrigible for me. So suppose we take a look at self-evidence. What is it? Under what conditions is a proposition self-evident? What kinds of propositions are self-evident? Examples would include very simple arithmetical truths such as

> (10) $2 + 1 = 3$,

simple truths of logic such as

> (11) no man is both married and unmarried,

perhaps the generalizations of simple truths of logic, such as

> (12) for any proposition p, the conjunction of p with its denial is false,

and certain propositions expressing identity and diversity; for example

> (13) Redness is distinct from greenness,

(14) the property of being prime is distinct from the property of being composite,

and

(15) the proposition *all men are mortal* is distinct from the proposition *all mortals are men.*[7]

There are others; Aquinas gives as examples

(16) the whole is greater than the part,

where, presumably, he means by 'part' what we mean by 'proper part', and, more dubiously,

(17) man is an animal.[8]

Still other candidates—candidates which may be less than entirely uncontroversial—come from many other areas; for example

(18) if p is necessarily true and p entails q, then q is necessarily true,

(19) if e^1 occurs before e^2 and e^2 occurs before e^3, then e^1 occurs before e^3,

and

(20) it is wrong to cause unnecessary (and unwanted) pain just for the fun of it.

What is it that characterizes these propositions? According to the tradition, the outstanding characteristic of a self-evident proposition is that one simply sees it to be true upon grasping or understanding it. Understanding a self-evident proposition is sufficient for apprehending its truth. Of course this notion must be relativized to *persons;* what is self-evident to you might not be to me. Very simple arithmetical truths will be self-evident to nearly all of us; but a truth like 17 + 18 = 35 may be self-evident only to some. And of course a proposition is self-evident to a person only if he does in fact grasp it; so a proposition will not be self-evident to those who do not apprehend the concepts involved in the proposition. As Aquinas says, some propositions are self-evident only to the learned; his example is the truth that immaterial substances do not occupy space. Among those propositions whose concepts not everyone grasps, some are such that anyone who *did* grasp them would see their truth; for example,

(21) A model of a first order theory T assigns truth to the axioms of T.

Others—17 + 13 = 30, for example—may be such that some but not all of those who apprehend them also see that they are true.

But how shall we understand this "seeing that they are true"? Those who speak of self-evidence explicitly turn to this visual metaphor and expressly explain self-evidence by reference to vision. There are two important aspects to the metaphor and two corresponding components to the idea of self-evidence. First, there is the *epistemic* component: a proposition p is self-evident to a person S only if S has *immediate* knowledge of p—i.e., knows p, and does not know p on the basis of his knowledge of other propositions. Consider a simple arithmetic truth such as 2 + 1 = 3 and compare it with one like 24 × 24 = 576. I know each of these propositions; and I know the second but not the first on the basis of computation, which is a kind of inference. So I have immediate knowledge of the first but not the second. The epistemic component of self-evidence, therefore, is immediate knowledge; it follows, of course, that any proposition self-evident to a person is true.

But there is also a phenomenological component. Consider again our two propositions; the first but not the second has about it a kind of luminous aura or glow when you bring it to mind or consider it. Locke speaks, in this connection, of an "evident luster"; a self-evident proposition, he says, displays a kind of "clarity and brightness to the attentive mind." Descartes speaks instead of "clarity and distinctness"; each, I think, is referring to the same phenomenological feature. And this feature is connected with another: Upon understanding a proposition of this sort one feels a strong inclination to accept it; this luminous obviousness seems to compel or at least impel assent. Aquinas and Locke, indeed, held that a person, or at any rate a normal well-formed human being, finds it impossible to withhold assent when considering a self-evident proposition. The phenomenological component of the idea of self-evidence, then, seems to have a double aspect: There is the luminous aura that *2 + 1 = 3* displays, and there is also an experienced tendency to accept or believe it. Perhaps, indeed, the luminous aura *just is* the experienced impulsion towards acceptance; perhaps these are the very same thing. In that case the phenomenological component would not have the double aspect I suggested it did have; in either case, however, we·must recognize this phenomenological aspect of self-evidence.

Now suppose we return to the main question: Why shouldn't belief in God be among the foundations of my noetic structure? Let us say that a proposition is *basic* for a person *S* if and only if it is in the foundations of *S*'s noetic structure; our question, then, is this: Can belief in God be properly basic for a person? If not, why not? The answer, on the part of our hypothetical Cliffordian, was that even if this belief is *true*, it does not have the characteristics a proposition must have to deserve a place in the foundations. There is no room in the foundations for a proposition that can be known only on the basis of other propositions. A proposition is properly basic for a person only if he knows it immediately—i.e., knows it, and does not know it on the basis of other propositions. The proposition that God exists, however, is at best truly believed, not known, and even if it were known, it wouldn't be known immediately. The only propositions that meet this condition of immediate knowledge are those that are self-evident or incorrigible. Since this proposition is neither, it is not properly basic for anyone; that is, no well-formed, rational noetic structure contains this proposition in its foundations.

But why should the theist concede these things? Suppose he grants that there is a foundation to his noetic structure: a set F of propositions such that (1) he knows each member of F *immediately* and (2) whatever else he knows is evident with respect to the members of F. Suppose he concedes, further, that he does know other things, and knows them on the basis of his knowledge of these basic propositions. Suppose, in a particularly irenic and conciliatory frame of mind, he concedes still further that much of what he believes, he believes but does not know; and that the rationality of these beliefs is to be tested or measured by way of their connections with those propositions that are basic for him. Why should he not combine these concessions with the claim that his belief in God is properly basic for him?

Because, says the Cliffordian, belief in God is neither self-evident nor incorrigible. But now we must look more closely at this fundamental principle of the foundationalist's position:

> (22) a proposition p is properly basic for a person S if and only if p is either self-evident to S or incorrigible for S;

that is, the foundations of a well-formed, rational noetic structure will contain propositions that are self-evident or incorrigible and will not contain any propositions that do not meet this condition.

We should note that self-evidence looms particularly large in the foundationalist scheme of things; in a way, his acceptance of what is incorrigible rests on self-evidence. For how does one know that a proposition *is* incorrigible for someone? How does one know that there are any incorrigible propositions at all? How does the foundationalist know that, e.g.,

> (23) S is in pain

is incorrigible for S? (23) is incorrigible for S if and only if it isn't possible that S mistakenly believe either (23) or its negation; and that *this* is so, if indeed it is so, is presumably, according to the foundationalist, itself self-evident. So self-evidence plays a peculiarly fundamental role for the foundationalist; a proposition is properly basic, he holds, only if it is self-evident or incorrigible; and that a given proposition falls into the latter category (if indeed it does) will be itself self-evident.

And here we must ask a question that has been clamoring for attention. How does the foundationalist know—how does anyone know—that, indeed, a given proposition *is* self-evident? How do we tell? Isn't it possible that a proposition should seem to me to be self-evident when in fact it is not? Consider an analogy. Suppose the theist claims that a proposition *p* is properly basic for a person *S* if *S* knows *p immediately;* and suppose he adds that one of the things he immediately knows is that God exists. The Cliffordian foundationalist, presumably, will want to reply as follows: you *say* you have immediate knowledge of this proposition, but perhaps you are mistaken; perhaps you only *believe* and do not *know* that God exists; perhaps, indeed, God does *not* exist. How do you know that you have immediate knowledge of this proposition? What leads you to think so?

Here the theist may be hard put to give an answer; but the foundationalist may find a similar question similarly embarrassing. How does he know that a given proposition—$7 + 5 = 12$, for example—*is* self-evident? Might we not be mistaken in our judgments of self-evidence? It seems obviously possible that there should be a race of persons—on some other planet, let's say— who think they find *other* propositions self-evident, some of these others being the denials of propositions *we* find self-evident. Perhaps this race invariably makes mistakes about what is self-evident. But might not the same thing be true of us? A proposition is self-evident, after all, only if it is *true;* and it certainly seems possible that we should believe a proposition self-evident when in fact it is not.

Nor need we rest content with the mere possibility that we should mistakenly find a proposition self-evident. Here the Russell paradoxes are peculiarly instructive. It seems self-evident to many that some properties—e.g., that of being a horse—do not exemplify themselves, while others—e.g., that of being a property—do. It seems self-evident, furthermore, that if some properties exemplify themselves and others do not, then there is such a property as *self-exemplification:* a property enjoyed by the properties in the first group but lacked by those in the second. But it also seems self-evident that if there is such a property as *self-exemplification*, then there is such a property as *non-self-exemplifiction:* the property a property has if and only if it does not exemplify itself. And of course it seems self-evident that if there is such a property as *non-self-exemplification*, then either it exemplifies itself or it does not. But if it does exemplify itself, it has the property of non-self-exemplification, in which case it does not exemplify itself. So if it does exemplify itself, it does not exemplify itself. But of course it is also true that if it does exemplify itself, then it does; so if it exemplifies itself, it both does and does not exemplify itself. Hence it does not exemplify itself. If, on the other hand, non-self-exemplification does not exemplify itself, then it does not have the property of non-self-exemplification, in which case it must have the property of self-exemplification, i.e., it exemplifies itself. So if it does not exemplify itself, it does exemplify itself. But it is also true that if it does not exemplify itself, then it does not exemplify itself; so if it does not exemplify itself, it both does and does not exemplify itself. Hence it is false that it does not exemplify itself, and true that it does. But now from propositions that seem self-evident we have deduced, by arguments that seem self-evidently right, that non-self-exemplification both exemplifies itself and does not exemplify itself; and this seems self-evidently false. The conclusions must be that at least one proposition that *seems* self-evident, is not *in fact* self-evident.

We must distinguish, therefore, what appears to be self-evident from what really is. Suppose we say that a proposition *seems* or *appears* self-evident to a person if he understands it, and if it displays the phenomenological feature referred to above—the "evident luster" of which Locke speaks—when he attentively considers it. How, then, does the foundationalist determine which propositions really *are* self-evident for him? By noting, of course, which ones appear self-evident to him; he has nothing else to go on. Of course he cannot sensibly hold that *whatever* appears self-evident, really is; that is the lesson of the Russell paradoxes. Perhaps, however, he can retreat to a weaker principle; perhaps he can hold that whatever seems self-evident has, as we might put it, the presumption of self-evidence in its favor. What appears to be self-evident ought to be taken to be self-evident unless there are reasons to the contrary—unless, for example, it appears self-evident that the proposition in question conflicts with *other* apparently self-evident propositions. And perhaps he will support this injunction by appeal to some such principles as

(24) Whatever seems self-evident is very likely true

or

(25) most propositions that *seem* self-evident *are* self-evident (and hence true).

But why should we accept (24) and (25)? Why does the foundationalist accept them? We should note, first of all, that neither of these propositions seems self-evident. One who understands them can nonetheless wonder whether they are true and in fact reject them. They do not possess that evident luster; and there certainly seem to be thinkable alternatives. Impressed with evolutionary theory, for example, we might suppose that the disposition to find these propositions self-evident is a trait emerging in the course of a long evolutionary development—a trait that has a certain survival value, but is at best fortuitously connected with truth, so that many or most of the propositions that appear self-evident to us are in fact false. Or, remembering our Descartes, we might speculate that we have been created by a being who delights in deception and produces in us a powerful tendency to accept certain false propositions as self-evident. Or we might speculate, in a Kierkegaardian vein, that our noetic endowment, once pristine and totally reliable, has been corrupted by some primal cataclysm befalling the human race. So (24) and (25) are not themselves apparently self-evident.

The important point here, however, lies in a different direction. Suppose these principles—(24) and (25)—*were* apparently self-evident. That is, suppose the proposition

(26) most propositions that display the phenomenological feature are true

itself displayed this feature. Would that be a relevant answer
to the question of what reason, if any, there is for believing
that most propositions displaying this feature are true? It is
hard to see how. The question is whether a proposition's
displaying this feature is a reason for thinking it true; to
reply that (26) itself displays this feature is simply to invite
the question again. Here the appeal to self-evidence seems
entirely unsatisfactory. It is as if the theist were to reply to
the question: "Why believe in God?" by pointing out that
God requires us to believe in Him, and requires us to believe
only what is true. This may indeed be so; but it does not supply a
reason for belief for anyone who does not already believe.
Similarly, the claim that (24) and (25) are apparently self-
evident, may or may not be true; but it can serve as a reason
for accepting them only for someone who already accepts
them. And hence it cannot serve as a reason, for the foundationalist, for accepting them.

The fact of the matter is, I think, that the foundationalist
has no reason at all for accepting (24) and (25). They do not
appear to be self-evident; and of course they are not incorrigible.
But if the foundationalist *does* have a reason for them, that
reason must trace back, ultimately, to the foundations; that
is, the foundationalist has a reason, on his own view, for (24)
and (25) only if they are evident with respect to propositions
that are properly basic for him—propositions that are self-
evident or incorrigible. It is hard to see how (24) or (25) could
be evident with respect to such propositions.

Accordingly, the foundationalist accepts (24) and (25) but
has no reason for so doing. He isn't *obliged* to accept them;
there are alternatives. He simply commits himself to them.
We might say that he commits himself to the trustworthiness
of his noetic equipment. More elegantly, he commits himself
to the reliability of his epistemic endowment. If, with an
older tradition, we think of reason as an organ, or power, or
faculty—the faculty whereby we discern what is self-evident—
then the foundationalist commits himself to the basic reliability
of reason. He doesn't do so, of course, as a result of (broadly
speaking) scientific or rational investigation; he does so in

advance of such investigation. For he has no reasons for accepting (24) and (25); but he does accept them, and he uses them to determine the acceptability of *other* propositions. In other words, (24) and (25) are members of the foundation of his noetic structure.

The foundationalist, therefore, commits himself to the basic reliability of reason. I do not say this by way of criticism; it is a commitment I share. The theist is by no means obliged to reject this commitment. Augustine, indeed, argued that reason is ultimately reliable just because God has created us and is not a deceiver. He has created us in such a way that certain propositions appear self-evident to us; and because he is a God of goodness and truth, he would not create us in such a way that *false* propositions should appear self-evident. Had Augustine been apprised of the Russell paradoxes, he might have expressed himself more guardedly; but his basic point remains. One who believes in God can certainly accept (24) and (25); and he, unlike the foundationalist, can give a reason for doing so.

Since the theist can properly concur with the foundationalist on (24) and (25), he can agree with the latter that apparently self-evident and incorrigible propositions are properly basic for S. But the foundationalist *credo,* we have seen, contains *two* elements, a positive and a negative. The foundationalist holds, positively, that

(27) self-evident and incorrigible propositions are properly basic for S,

and he adds, negatively, that

(28) *only* propositions of those sorts are properly basic for S.

But why should we accept this negative element? What is there to be said in favor of it? Do we have anything more than the foundationalist's word for (28)?

The fact is we have *less* than the foundationalist's word for it. For, as we have seen, it seems that he himself accepts (24) and (25) as basic; these are among the foundations of his noetic

structure. But (24) and (25) are neither self-evident nor incorrigible; hence he appears to be hoist with his own petard. A
similar point may be made with respect to (28) itself. (28) is
neither self-evident nor incorrigible; nor does it appear to
follow from propositions that are. It is, however, basic for the
foundationalist. So he holds that self-evident and incorrigible
propositions are the only viable candidates for the foundations of his noetic structure, but he himself accepts as basic
(24) or (25), and (28), none of which meets this condition. But
suppose we waive this point for the moment and leave the
foundationalist to try to see how to achieve coherence here.
Is there any reason to believe (28)? If so, what is it? (28) certainly
does not appear to be self-evident; it is certainly not incorrigible. It is very hard to see, furthermore, that it either follows
from or is evident with respect to propositions that *are* self-
evident or incorrigible. So it is hard to see that there is any
reason for accepting (28), even from a roughly foundationalist
point of view. Why then should we accept it? Why should the
theist feel any obligation to believe it?

The answer, I believe, is that there is no reason at all for
accepting (28); it is no more than a bit of intellectual imperi-
alism on the part of the foundationalist. He means to commit
himself to reason and to nothing more; he therefore declares
irrational any noetic structure that contains more—belief in
God, for example—in its foundations. But here there is no
reason for the theist to follow his example; the believer is not
obliged to take his word for it. So far we have found no reason
at all for excluding belief in God from the foundations; so far
we have found no reason at all for believing that belief in God
cannot be basic in a rational noetic structure. To accept belief
in God as basic is clearly not irrational in the sense of being
proscribed by reason or in conflict with the deliverances of
reason. The dictum that belief in God is not basic in a rational
noetic structure is neither apparently self-evident nor apparently incorrigible. Nor does it seem to be a deductive consequence of what is self-evident or incorrigible. Is there, then,
any reason at all for holding that a noetic structure including
belief in God as basic is irrational? If there is, it remains to
be specified.

It is worth noting, by way of conclusion, that the mature believer, the mature theist, does not typically accept belief in God tentatively, or hypothetically, or until something better comes along. Nor, I think, does he accept it as a conclusion from other things he believes; he accepts it as basic, as a part of the foundations of his noetic structure. The mature theist *commits* himself to belief in God; this means that he accepts belief in God as basic. Our present inquiry suggests that there is nothing contrary to reason or irrational in so doing.

NOTES

1. "Evil and Omnipotence," *Mind* 64 (1955), pp. 203-4.
2. See, for example, T. McPherson, *The Philosophy of Religion* (London: D. Van Nostrand, 1965); T. Penelhum, *Religion and Rationality* (New York: Random House, 1958); J. Ross, *Philosophical Theology* (Indianapolis: Bobbs Merrill, 1969); A. Plantinga, *God and Other Minds* (Ithaca, N.Y.: Cornell University Press, 1967), and numerous others.
3. See my book *The Nature of Necessity* (Oxford: Clarendon Press, 1974), chap. 1.
4. W. K. Clifford, "The Ethics of Belief," from *Lectures and Essays* (London: Macmillan, 1879).
5. *Theory of Knowledge*, 1st ed. (Englewood Cliffs, N.J.: Prentice-Hall, 1966), p. 34.
6. Philip Quinn has pointed out (in correspondence) that, according to (9), *false* propositions will be incorrigible for me now: Although I do not now seem to see something green, the proposition *I seem to see something green* is incorrigible for me now. I'm not certain this feature of the definition is a defect; if it is, it can be repaired by adding the clause '*p* is true' to the *definiens* or, as Quinn suggests, by adding '*S* believes *p* at *t*'.
7. Examples of these kind are given by Locke, *Essay Concerning Human Understanding*, Book IV, chap. 7.
8. ST 1, Q1 a 2; SCG I, chap. 10.

Rationality and Religious Belief
—A Perverse Question

GEORGE I. MAVRODES

Is religion rational? The theme of this volume invites us to consider this question. It is not the perverse question to which my title refers; that comes later. But I think it is a hard question. Maybe it is hard in the sense that it is hard to find out what its true answer is. But it is also hard in another way —hard to understand, hard to see what the point of it is. And maybe—I now suspect this to be a fact—when we uncover its point it turns out to be not a very important question.

At the outset, the question seems to invite some rather straightforward clarifications and restrictions. In the first place, there are a lot of religions and there have been even more. Perhaps they are not all the same with respect to rationality. We should begin, perhaps, with a somewhat narrower question, a question about some particular religion. So I might most usefully focus upon my own religion, Christianity. Is it rational?

The theme of this volume seems to invite us to limit our concern even further. The notion of rationality is applied to several different aspects of human life—there are philosophical discussions of rational action, for example, and of rational desires. But our theme here connects rationality and belief. And so my own discussion here will be limited to this aspect. What I will call 'the rationality question' is the question of whether religious *belief*, rather than religion overall, is rational. And now, combining these two limitations, we find ourselves with the question of whether Christian belief is rational. For illustrative purposes, I will sometimes refer to a single, fairly specific and fairly important belief, the belief that there exists a God who created the world. A typical version of the rationality question would then ask whether this, which I here call 'theistic belief,' is a rational belief.

When I began to think about writing this paper I thought that this was a reasonably straightforward question and also that I knew the answer to it. Of course Christian belief, and that element in it which I have called 'theistic belief,' is rational. (After all, it is my own belief!) And so I began to cast about for what I might say in support of that judgment in some useful and illuminating way. Now, however, I am not as sure as I was that theistic belief is rational after all, at least in a plain and straightforward way. Let me, therefore, approach this topic somewhat obliquely.

Many philosophers have produced arguments intended to prove, at least so it seems to me, that theistic belief is *true*. St. Thomas is a classic example of this orientation. He concludes a well-known argument with the words "Therefore it is necessary to arrive at a first mover, moved by no other; and this everyone understands to be God." Another argument ends with "Therefore some intelligent being exists by whom all natural things are directed to their end; and this being we call God." And so on. In this orientation Thomas has a host of companions, both philosophers and others.

In order to have the orientation which I am here identifying one need not, however, proceed by way of argumentation. For there may be other ways of determining whether theistic belief is true. (In fact, it seems to me, unless there is some other way of determining the truth of some propositions, argument itself would be useless for determining the truth of any proposition.) So a person who was concerned with Christianity might seek to have—or maybe he will have without seeking it—a mystical experience or an instance of divine revelation which bears on the truth of theistic belief. Or maybe something else will happen to him which seems to him relevant, perhaps sufficient, for determining the truth value of theistic belief.

Such an approach also belongs to the orientation I am here identifying.

Furthermore, I construe this approach to philosophizing about religion to include as well all those arguments, experiences, etc., which are adduced to show that theistic belief is *false*. For convenience, we may say that all of these attempts are *truth-oriented*.

Not every philosophical treatment of religion seems to be truth-oriented, in the sense of claiming to determine, even probabilistically, the truth value of theistic belief or some other substantive religious belief. Alvin Plantinga's brilliant book *God and Other Minds* provides a useful contrast with Thomas. He examines some Thomistic arguments, as well as several other theistic and atheistic arguments, and finds them all seriously defective. But that examination constitutes only what we might think of as a sub-routine in the book. The book as a whole does not profess to be about the truth of theistic belief, but about something else—its rationality. It begins with these sentences:

> In this study I shall investigate the rational justifiability of a particular religious belief—the belief in the existence of God as He is conceived in the Judeo-Christian tradition. But the question arises: how can one approach this topic? How could one show that it is or is not rational to believe in God's existence?

He ends that book with the sentences:

> Hence my tentative conclusion: if my belief in other minds is rational, so is my belief in God. But obviously the former is rational; so, therefore, is the latter.

In the introduction Plantinga promises an investigation into the rationality of theistic belief and suggests that he will be concerned to "show" that it is, or is not, rational. The concluding sentences claim the completion of this project. They set forth his "tentative conclusion"—presumably supported by the argument of the 270 intervening pages—that his belief in God is rational. Well, perhaps Plantinga is right. Maybe his belief is rational. Here, however, I cite his work only as an example of what we might call the *rationality-oriented* approach. One who uses this approach sets himself primarily to determine whether theistic belief is, or is not, rational.

Now, I have so far talked as though some people proceeded in the truth-oriented way and others in the rationality-oriented way. But, if it is possible to proceed in these ways at all, there is nothing to prevent someone from doing both. He might, like Thomas, seek and find arguments which have propositions expressing theistic belief for their conclusions, and he might also, like Plantinga, seek and find arguments which have propositions about the rationality of theistic belief for their conclusions. Let us suppose that there is someone who does this. What results might he get?

Here, it seems to me, a common assumption about rationality becomes very important. People who use the notion of rationality a good deal generally take it for granted that a belief need not be true in order to be rational and that it need not be false in order to be irrational. (We might note, as perhaps an example of this assumption in action, that Plantinga, in *God and Other Minds*, did not claim to prove that his belief in God was true before concluding that it was rational. Nor, having concluded that it was rational, did he draw from that the further conclusion that it was true.) This fact about rationality, if indeed it is a fact, seems to me to be one of great importance. We can begin by drawing up a list of some of the possible combinations of truth value and rationality for a certain belief, p. For convenience, let us use the expression 'Rp' as an abbreviation of the sentence 'the belief that p is a rational belief.' First, then, we get two combinations in which the virtues seem to coincide as they should in the best of all possible worlds. I call these the "good" combinations. They are:

(1) p and Rp.

and

(2) Not-p and not-Rp.

There are, however, also some interesting "perverse" combinations. These include:

(3) p and not-Rp.
(4) p and R (not-p).

and

(5) Not-p and Rp.

(3) and (4) may initially be thought to be equivalent, but it is not clear that they are. If p is a belief such that both it and its negation are rational, then (4) does not entail (3). If p is a belief such that neither it nor its negation is rational, then (3) does not entail (4). Are there any such beliefs? The answer is part of a further analysis of rationality, and I don't now know what it is. But even if (3) and (4) are equivalent no harm is done (except to elegance) by letting them both stand.

Now, we were thinking about a person who sought to determine both the truth and the rationality of theistic belief, and we asked what results he might get. He might, of course, end up with one of the good combinations—i.e., he might prove combination (1) or (2). If so, then no special problems, as least of the sort I want to consider here, arise. But the perverse possibilities are more troublesome and maybe more interesting.

Imagine, for example, that our philosophical friend comes up with a conclusive argument to the effect that God exists and another conclusive argument to the effect that theistic belief is not rational. That is, he proves combination (3). One can get much the same effect, I think, by imagining that he develops strong evidence, though not conclusive evidence, for each of the conjuncts in (3). Or suppose he proves combination (4), that God exists but that atheistic belief is rational. Or, if you prefer, you can get roughly the same perversity out of supposing that he establishes combination (5). What bearing are these proofs supposed to have on his beliefs? One way of putting it is to ask whether he shall be atheist, theist, or agnostic. But another way is to ask whether he will opt for truth or for rationality. That is the perverse question to which my title refers.

Some of you, I think, will want to resist this perverse question from the outset on the grounds that the perverse situations to which it refers are really impossible. Well, maybe they are. But why? The combinations themselves seem to be generally accepted as possible. Indeed, I would suppose, some people think them not only possible but not all that uncommon. And anyway, common or uncommon, if the combinations are possible, then they may actually occur. And if they do occur, then why should there not be a proof that they have occurred? If there cannot be such a proof, at least the reason for this failure cannot be that the proposition to be proved is impossible, or even that it is false.

Other reasons might be adduced for the impossibility of the proofs I have imagined, and I want to consider some of them soon. But before that, let me say that I have no objection to answering the perverse question for myself. If push comes to shove, I think I would opt for truth over rationality every time. Or perhaps I should put it more cautiously. I think that in some sense or other that would be the right way to choose, the way one ought to choose, and I hope that I would make that choice every time.

Maybe someone will suggest that I choose in this way because I do not have a high enough regard for rationality. Well, maybe I do not. But that fact, if it is a fact, could be a consequence rather than a cause of (or reason for) the judgment I expressed above. Maybe I have a lower regard for rationality because I have already judged that it must play second fiddle to truth. Anyway, at the moment I don't have anything very incisive to say in favor of that judgment, though something may develop out of the following discussion. But I continue to recommend this question to those who are interested in rationality. Which would you choose, if you were faced with one of the perverse possibilities? And why?

Now, it may well be that some of you still feel that what I have called the perverse combinations really are perverse, in some way which entails that we should not consider them to be real possibilities, and that we therefore need not concern ourselves with the perverse question which depends upon them.

And perhaps you are right. They certainly seem to me to have something queer about them. What might it be?

In this last part of this paper I want to suggest and explore two different conjectures, both of which will block the perverse question. The first conjecture is this:

> (C1) Sentences of the form, "the belief that p is a rational belief," do not express propositions and have no truth value at all.

The claim that this conjecture is true might be called "the non-cognitivist theory of rationality." And this theory may, for all I know, be true. If it is true then the perverse combinations cannot be proved (nor, for that matter, can the good combinations) because what appears to be the second conjunct in those combinations is not a proposition and has no truth value at all. If one were to hold this theory, then (I suppose) the most plausible account to be given of rationality sentences is that they are used to express the speaker's approval of the beliefs to which rationality is ascribed and his disapproval of beliefs to which irrationality is ascribed. If that is the case, then those of us who like theistic belief could go on saying that it is rational, and those who dislike it could say it is irrational. But it would be rather obtuse for either of us to marshall arguments or evidence to show or prove that it is rational or irrational. Rather (if we concern ourselves with proofs or evidence at all) we should shift from the rationality-oriented approach to the truth-oriented approach, adducing whatever arguments and evidence we can find which bear upon the truth of theistic belief.

The non-cognitivist theory of rationality is not, however, the only possibility which we might canvass at this point. Consider the following conjecture:

> (C2) While a proposition might be true and irrational, or untrue and rational, nevertheless a proposition for which there is a proof is thereby rendered rational, and one for which there is a counter-proof is thereby rendered irrational.

And we might extend this conjecture to cover the probabilistic cases by saying that if there is evidence (all the available evidence?) which renders a given proposition probable (a probability greater than 0.5?), then that proposition is thereby rendered rational, and similarly for irrationality. Then the trouble with the perverse combinations would be that, while they might be true, there could not be a proof, or perhaps even a balance of evidence, that they were true, for the production of a proof for the first conjunct would render the second conjunct false. And thus we will never be faced with the perverse question.

This conjecture seems to me to have a lot of initial appeal, and I want to look at it in more than one way. One of its interesting facets is this. The conjecture entails that there may be propositions which are true and yet, in some strong sense, incapable of proof. Are there any such propositions? I used to think there were not, but now the matter seems less clear. Consider, as perhaps a less problematic case, the following:

(6) p and there is never a proof of p.

There is some plausibility in supposing that there may be some proposition, p, which is true though never proved. (This is, of course, different from the claim that it is impossible to prove p.) If there is such a proposition, then some proposition having the form of (6) is true. But it would seem that no proposition having the form of (6) could ever be proved—not merely that it will never be proven, but that, in some strong sense, it is impossible to prove a proposition such as (6). For in order to prove (6) we should both have to prove p and also prove that there is no proof of p. And so it would seem that the entailment I noted above is OK. Or is it?

Consider the following, which might be put forward as a "theorem," "principle," or something of the sort, bearing on the notion of a proof:

(7) For any p and q, if there is a proof of the proposition p *and* q then there is a proof of p.

Now, if (7) is true, then (6) is unprovable. But what seems more interesting, to me at least, is this. When I make (7) explicit, then I think of the possibility of rejecting it. And if I reject it, at least hypothetically, then most of the plausibility seems to evaporate from the claim that (6) could be both true and unprovable.

Perhaps I can make that clearer by substituting, for a moment, the notion of an argument for that of a proof. And suppose that we use a rather minimal notion of an argument—that of an ordered set of propositions, one of which is marked as the conclusion. Now, there may easily be, and often will be, arguments which have conjunctions as their conclusions without having the first conjunct, or any propostion equivalent to the first conjunct, as their conclusions. In fact, in many such arguments the first conjunct will not appear as a line anywhere in the argument. And in cases where the conjunction is true there may readily be *sound* arguments which have this conjunction for their conclusion without having the first conjunct as their conclusion, or even as a line in the argument.

Returning now to proofs, many proofs seem to be associated with arguments in such a way that what is proved is the conclusion of the associated argument. But then, I wonder, why should there not be a proof of (6) which is associated with an argument which has (6) for its conclusion but does not have p for its conclusion? And when I ask myself that question it no longer seems to me so clear that propositions having the form of (6) must be unprovable.

At this point someone may think of proposing the following principle as an analogue of (7):

> (8) For any p and q, if there is an argument which has *p and q* for its conclusion then there is an argument which has p for its conclusion.

And he may then argue that if there were to be a proof of (6) of the sort which I imagined above, there would also be a proof of p associated with the argument which (8) guarantees to exist.

Is (8) true? That depends, I think, on what is necessary for there to *be* an argument. If we take an argument to be a sort of historical entity, something which has to be invented by someone, as Anselm may be thought to have invented the ontological argument, with the propositions being actually thought of and put into order by some human being at some time and place, then it strikes me as unlikely that (8) is true. The vagaries of human thought seem to be against it. On this interpretation of what it is for there to be an argument, then, the line of reasoning which depends on (8) would seem to fail.

If, however, we construe an argument as a kind of "eternal object," a possible arrangement, say, of possible assertions, then (8) is true. In fact, a stronger claim is true:

> (9) For and p and q, if there is a sound argument which has p *and* q for its conclusion then there is a sound argument which has p for its conclusion.

If we suppose, as the reasoner we are here considering seems to suppose, that every such argument either constitutes or is associated with a proof of its conclusion, then (9) will indeed guarantee that (6) is unprovable. Unfortunately, it will also guarantee that (6) is false. For, in the sense required by (9), if p is true then there will be a sound argument with p for its conclusion. Consequently, there will be a proof of p. Therefore, for every p, either p is false or there is a proof of p. And hence every proposition having the form of (6) is false. Construing arguments, then, as eternal objects will not support the thesis that (6) may be both true and unprovable.

Now, we got into the digression, as you will remember, because we were considering the conjecture that the production of a proof for a certain proposition would render that proposition rational, etc., and that therefore we could never have a proof of, or perhaps even evidence for, the perverse combinations. This thesis, I said, entails the claim that there can be propositions which are both true and unprovable. The best candidate I can think of for his role, however—proposition (6)—seems to depend upon (7). And while I am not sure that (7) is false, I also do not think of any strong reason for accepting it as true. So I find myself not in a very strong position vis-à-vis the conjecture which we were considering.

Nevertheless, conjecture (C2) continues to strike us, at least in some moods, as very attractive. If we accept it as true, then we need trouble ourselves no more about the perverse question. But how else does it bear on religious belief?

That depends, I think, on how we construe such things as there being a proof of a proposition, or there being a certain amount and quality of evidence for a proposition. Sometimes we talk as if there either were or were not a proof of a certain thesis, or as if there either were or were not a certain amount of evidence for it, and that is the end of the matter. And this, in turn, leads us to think and act as if these proofs, evidence, etc., were eternal entities and relations, independent of such historical and variable factors as the beliefs of actual people. If we do construe things in this way, then one serious problem which we face is that of identifying just what eternal object or relation we mean by terms such as 'proof' and 'evidence.' If, for example, we were to identify the proof of a proposition with a sound argument for that proposition, construing the argument as itself an eternal and non-historical object, then we would have made a reasonably clear identification. Unfortunately, however, there is, in this sense, a sound argument for every true proposition, and no sound argument for any false proposition. Consequently, on this interpretation the notions of truth and rationality will be extensionally equivalent. It will not be the case, as seems generally assumed, that a belief could be rational and false, or irrational but true. And so this identification is probably unsatisfactory. Maybe someone has a more promising candidate. I do not know what it is.

Supposing, however, that a better candidate is put forward, we should have to deal with a second problem. Given that this eternal object or relation does not guarantee the truth of the proposition with which it is associated (and that its absence does not guarantee falsehood), why should we concern ourselves with it *in connection with decisions about what to believe?* If I am troubled about whether to be a theist, why should I concern myself with whether the proposition *There is a God*, etc., is associated with some eternal object called a 'proof', or with the rationality which that association may generate. And we must not assume, just because the word 'rationality' has been attached to this association, that there is bound to be a genuine relevance. For all I know, every proposition may be associated with several eternal objects and relations which have no bearing at all upon its believability. And we cannot make these things relevant merely by attaching to them names such as 'proof' or 'rationality'.

Well, I have not much confidence in that project, though perhaps someone will surprise me here by his success in it. We might, however, proceed in another direction. Instead of construing (C2) in terms of eternal objects and relations, we might understand it in terms of historical and biographical achievements. If we want to make this move terminologically explicit, we might replace talk of there being a proof of p with the claim that someone has proved p to someone (perhaps himself), and we could replace talk about there being evidence for p with the claim that someone (perhaps ourselves) has evidence for p. This way of understanding (C2) has the advantage that it allows for the possibility that something may be true and irrational, or rational and false. It can also be worked out so that rationality seems to bear upon whether something "ought" to be believed, whether it is intellectually OK to believe it, etc. But only with a certain restriction.

Assume for the moment that there is a God. Then the following sequence of events seems possible: A certain medieval monk invents a sound argument for the existence of God and proves His existence to his atheistically inclined brother-in-law. Soon thereafter both the monk and his brother-in-law die of bubonic plague, and the only copy of the argument is destroyed in a fire which consumes the monastery library. Now, it certainly looks as though that series of events might occur without my knowing anything about it, without my ever hearing of that argument, etc. And it is hard to see how the mere occurrence of this series of events, without my knowledge, could have any bearing upon whether I ought to believe in God, whether it is intellectually OK for me to be a theist. It seems unlikely that such events could, of themselves, make my belief rational. Of course, on some plausible construals of what a proof involves, such events could not occur unless God exists. If so, then if they occur and I believe in God, then I have a true belief. But for any true proposition at all, regardless of whether anyone proves it, if I believe that proposition I will have a true belief. Trying to connect rationality and proof in this way by means of truth will have the result of making rationality and truth extensionally equivalent. But that is presumably unsatisfactory.

It looks, then, as though the monk's success in inventing a proof of the existence of God, and in proving the existence of God to his brother-in-law, cannot of itself make my belief in God rational. Perhaps it made *his* belief rational, or that of his brother-in-law. But even if I have the same belief they had—i.e., I believe the same proposition—it does not make my belief rational. *My* having a proof might do that for me. But his having one cannot. If, then, we construe the notions of proof and evidence that occur in conjecture (C2) in this historical and biographical way, they may turn out to have some important bearing on rationality. But then it looks as though the notion of rationality must also be construed historically and biographically.

One way of putting the latter point is this. Rationality claims are often ambiguous, subject to at least two interpretations. Consider

(10) My belief that God exists is rational.

This may be construed as predicating rationality of the proposition that I believe, as in

(11) The proposition *God exists*, which is one that I believe, is a rational proposition.

Or it may be taken to predicate rationality of my believing, as in

(12) My believing that God exists is rational.

Now, if we want to connect rationality with notions like proof and evidence in the way suggested by (C2), and if we construe proof and evidence historically and biographically, then it looks as though we must construe rationality statements along the lines indicated by (12) rather than by (11). We must predicate (or deny) rationality of a certain person's believing, rather than of the content of his belief. And thus different people may share the content of their belief, but differ in the rationality of their believings.

Conjecture (C2), then, interpreted in this way, seems to provide us with a coherent and not totally implausible way of avoiding the troublesome perverse question of the early part of this paper. It seems to me, however, that in its turn it gives rise to another troublesome query, one with which we may end. When rationality is construed in this way, is there any importance in investigating and settling rationality questions? My own guess is that they are of no great importance at all. Plantinga, we remember, claimed that his belief in God was rational. Is it of any importance for me to find out whether he was correct in this claim? Not that I can see. Can my judgment about the rationality of Plantinga's believing have any proper bearing upon my own decision to be theist or atheist? It is hard to see how it can, since, as we have already noted several times, we want to construe rationality in such a way that it is compatible with falsehood and irrationality compatible with truth. To make Plantinga's rationality relevant to my believing is to open the door to the perverse possibilities all over again.

But even if it is not very important for me to determine whether Plantinga is rational in his believings, might it not be important for me to determine whether my own belief (or prospective belief) is (or would be) rational? Well, maybe. But how? Suppose that I consider becoming an atheist. And suppose also that I determine that if I were to have the atheistic belief I would be believing rationally. How can that determination bear—or how should it bear—on the conduct of my intellectual life? If I have also determined, either independently or in conjunction with the first determination, that atheistic belief is true, then the first determination seems to add nothing relevant. I will, or at least it seems I should, become an atheist on the basis of the second determination. Conjecture (C2) rules out the possibility that I could have determined that atheism is false. But maybe it allows that I might determine that my being an atheist would be rational without my gathering any balance of evidence at all either for or against the truth of atheism. Could I—should I—hold the atheistic belief because it is rational, even though I know that I have no reason at all to think that it is true rather than false? I seem to find no attraction in that prospect at all. But if someone does feel such an attraction and can do anything to bring that attractiveness to light, then maybe we can get further on this topic.

Faith, Belief, and the Problem of Rationality in Religion

JOHN E. SMITH

The relation between faith and reason was a problem for Christianity from the start and has continued to present itself in ever new forms over the succeeding centuries, including our own. The reason behind this fact is important for every discussion of the problem. Unlike some of the Oriental traditions in which the religious and philosophical strands were often so interwoven as to be virtually indistinguishable from each other, the Western religions encountered the *autonomous* philosophical traditions of the ancient Greek thinkers and thus had to relate their religious insights to a *logos* which came, as it were, from the outside. The positive side of the encounter is manifest in the enterprise of theology itself, the attempt to express primary religious experience and insight with *conceptual clarity* and *systematic coherence*. In establishing theological traditions, the church fathers felt themselves bound by high standards of rationality, even if there were difference of opinion among them as to how that rationality was to be understood in its nature and its scope.

As a result of this ancient encounter between religious and philosophical traditions, *three* polar tensions developed in the succeeding centuries. Since my focus is not historical, but philosophical, I shall limit my comments on the first two in order to concentrate on the third, which, as I shall point out, defines our present situation. I do not, however, believe that we can fully understand that situation if we approach it without any historical perspective whatever. The first polarity developed inside the household of faith between those like Augustine and Anselm who adhered to the program of "faith seeking understanding" and thus insisted on some form of *continuity* between rationality and the content of faith and those like Tertullian and the later opponents of dialectic who insisted on the essential *discontinuity* between religious insight and all forms of rational mediation. It is important to notice that for those adopting the first position, the understanding in question was meant to illuminate and confirm a faith in which people already participated and not to propel them, so to speak, into faith *ab initio*.[1] The adherents of the discontinuity view, on the other hand, insisted on the utter uniqueness and even "absurdity" of faith when seen from the perspective of an external rationality and for two reasons. First, in their view the ultimate mystery represented by the religious content defies rational articulation, and, secondly, adjusting faith to rational demands results either in its distortion or subordination to secular thought, or in self-deceptive attempts to avoid the embarrassments stemming from the fact that, viewed rationally, Christianity is "absurd."

The second polarity, also one which made its appearance *within* the household of faith, found its roots in the essential ambiguity which exists in the religious concept of faith derivative from the Bible. This ambiguity is quite unmistakable as manifested, on the one hand, in the faith of Abraham or Job, which meant trust in God, come what may, and, on the other hand, in the faith of Paul or John, which meant the belief that God is love, that love "never faileth," and that the life and death of Jesus were the ultimate manifestation of that love. The polar tension is between what can be called the *conative* side of faith, where the emphasis falls on the personal relations of trust, dependence, commitment, devotion together with the experience of presence, and the *cognitive* side, where the emphasis falls on ideational content and the claim that there are distinctive truths about God, man, and the world of nature that are essential for the religious outlook. The seriousness and even

potentially destructive character of this polarity becomes most
clear through consideration of the uncompromising critiques
made by the proponents of each view against the other. De-
fenders of the *conative* side of faith seek to identify it exclusively
as a personal relationship, an experience of presence, an encounter with God, a being grasped by the intrinsic power of a
person who reveals the divine nature. Faith, so understood,
stands strictly opposed to a "propositional attitude," which
is appropriate for belief but not for faith in the specifically
religious sense. On this view, faith as personal relationship
coincides with some form of "acquaintance" and is contrasted
with the holding of "propositions about" some object of belief.

Proponents of the *cognitive* dimension of faith insist that
conceptual content is essential for meaning and understanding
in religion, and that without such content, faith becomes
"blind" in the twofold sense of lacking form and direction
and of being without rational foundations. The central claim
made in behalf of this view is that if faith is to be shared and
communicated within a religious community, it must be made
intelligible, something which is impossible if "propositions
about" are totally excluded either as illegitimate or as expressive
merely of a "belief" which is not faith.

The potentially tragic character of this polarity, in addition
to the fact of its having arisen within the household of faith,
is that the tension stems from the basic ambiguity in the biblical conception of faith itself, and both positions contain an
element of truth which must not be lost. Unhappily, neither
position is able to do justice to the element of truth in the other
insofar as each insists on understanding faith as exclusively
conative or cognitive. That both positions, however, are inadequate when set in polar opposition can readily be shown.
On the one hand, the Bernards, the Luthers, the Jonathan
Edwardses, the Schleiermachers and the Kierkegaards can point
to the undeniably personal and experiential character of religious faith as trust in God, the main source of courage, hope,
and joy amidst the evils and contingencies of human life. They
can call attention to the insufficiency of a purely "notional"

or intellectual understanding of, and assent to, theological doctrines for the central religious aim of affecting the will and transforming the person. Against the exclusively cognitive conception of faith, they can insist that on such a view only theologians and dialecticians would be truly religious and that religion becomes identified with the holding of correct doctrine. And to this extent the proponents of the conative interpretation are right; both the history and phenomenology of religion in man's experience show that a purely intellectualistic construction of faith is forced to leave out much that is essential.

On the other hand, however, the Origens, the Augustines, the Anselms, the Abelards, the Scotuses, and the Aquinases can point to the necessity of ideational content as the only means of expressing what is believed, including in what or in whom one trusts, and of making faith intelligible. The demand for intelligibility points in two directions at once. There is, first, the need to have a conceptual and intersubjective symbol for the content of faith as the basis for a religious community. Second, this content must be related to the other areas and dimensions of experience and knowledge if religion is not to become an esoteric domain which neither influences or is influenced by the culture in which it exists. Both of these demands for intelligibility are rooted in something essential to the nature of religion itself: Religious faith or insight is always an interpreting *word* or an expression of the significance, purpose, and intent of human life. This truth about religion becomes abundantly clear in times of religious awakenings, renewals, and revivals, when numerous forms of "enthusiasm" appear and the critical mind is overwhelmed by a proliferation of "experiences" which cannot be understood or interpreted without appeal to concepts and doctrines. Let faith be as intimately connected with the being and center of the person as you please,[2] it ceases to have the distinctive meaning it must have if it receives no conceptual expression and implies no knowledge about the reality or realities trusted or believed in. For those who emphasize the cognitive aspect of faith, the total opposition of faith and belief is seen as an exaggeration and the supposition that there can be acquaintance, encounter, and the experience of presence without "propositions about" is regarded as illusion.

Leaving aside the question as to whether there is a way of reconciling or harmonizing these two aspects of faith, it seems clear enough that neither one is adequate taken by itself and that both aspects are essential. For without the conative element faith becomes lifeless and inert, failing to achieve its religious function, in Whitehead's fine expression, of "cleansing the inward parts." Without the cognitive element, however, faith likewise is incomplete, because loss of the interpreting word leaves it inarticulate and forever on the verge of a collapse into an immediacy which defies both intelligibility and the possibility of critical appraisal.

Yet a third polarity has developed in relation to religion and rationality, and while it is clearly connected with the previous two, it manifests an absolutely fundamental difference from them. Earlier on, I claimed that this polarity defines for the most part our present religious situation and that consequently I would devote the major part of this discussion to it. Before attempting to fulfill that promise, however, I want to underline the point previously made about the first two polarities having developed *within* the confines of what I called the household of faith and what Tillich called the theological circle. The polar tension between those who argued for continuity between faith and rationality and those who insisted on an essential discontinuity between the two, and the polar tension just set forth between the proponents of the conative and cognitive aspects of faith represent two polarities of interpretation by parties within the Christian tradition. The differences of opinion, profound and seemingly irreconcilable as they are, must be understood as domestic quarrels, so to speak. The protagonists all participated in the Christian faith and its traditions, and all, in some sense and to some degree, accepted this faith as something they were attempting to understand, to articulate correctly, or to preserve from misinterpretation and distortion. Neither of these polarities can be correctly described as disputes between Christians and non-Christians, because all parties involved regarded themselves as adherents to the Christian faith and, despite their differences, there was little tendency for anyone to suppose that the struggle was between Christians, on the one side, and nonbelievers or outside secular critics, on the other. This point is of crucial importance, especially for appreciating the force of the third polar tension to be considered, because it is by no means a domestic affair taking place within the community of those who presuppose basic Christian convictions. The modern problems of rationality in religion has been set largely by the decline, beginning in the eighteenth century, of the classical philosophical traditions, coupled with the rise of a new conception of rationality which has been determined by three factors; first, the norms operative in experimental science; secondly, a logic which purports to be entirely formal and thus independent of particular philosophical commitments; and, finally, a technical and instrumental, as distinct from a reflective and speculative, reason. The third polarity is between this new and largely secular standard of rationality on the one side and the religious tradition—usually represented by the nature and use of its language or by some single belief taken to be typical—on the other.

It should be clear that this polarity, unlike the others mentioned, is no intramural affair and for three reasons. First, theologians, up to and including the time of Scotus and Ockham, worked through the medium of a reason which had an ontological foundation and was thus congenial to various forms of rational theology based on the coordination of the concepts of Being and God. Rationality in religion was a function of this ontological reason, and large differences of opinion within that framework were allowed. In this sense, the widely divergent view of, for example, Anselm and Ockham were both regarded as "rational," and those whose bent was either nondialectical or anti-dialectical were not styled "irrational" but rather devotional, moral, meditative, or mystical. By contrast, the modern conception of rationality is either non-ontological or anti-ontological in orientation. It is rooted in a *Scientia* which has little or no room for what was traditionally included under *Sapientia*, and considerations drawn from religious experience and insight have played no part in the determination of what this rationality means. In our situation, for the most part, to raise the problem of rationality in religion is to ask whether it is "rational" in terms of this extramural conception or standard, a very different matter from the classical enterprise of determining whether the content of faith could be made intelligible in terms of an essentially philosophically oriented conception of rationality.

Two other factors are also significant for understanding the polarity under discussion. One is that in the traditional situation, the *possiblity* of showing that the content of faith could be made intelligible was a *real* possibility, even if it could not always be realized to the satisfaction of all concerned; whereas in the modern situation, for many at least, no such possibility is envisaged at all, because the standard of rationality has been defined for the specific purpose of excluding it. I do not believe that this need be so, but that it has been the case in the recent past cannot be denied. The second factor concerns the status of the religious tradition in the polarity and the manner in which it is represented. Very frequently, the problem of the rationality of religious belief is approached by taking a single belief such as the Last Judgment or Eternal Life, ignoring its peculiar religious and theological significance in the context of a tradition of faith, and then asking whether it is "rational" to hold that belief, using as criterion the totally alien conception of rationality just indicated. Sometimes, moreover, the question is posed even more abstractly, and we are asked to decide whether, assuming that some agreement can be reached as to what constitutes a belief as "religious," religious belief as such is rational or not. I am not for the moment at least passing critical judgment (except perhaps by implication) on this way of dealing with the matter. My aim is rather to understand as clearly as possible the present climate of opinion and how very different it is from situations in the past. Asking for the rationality of religion on the current scene is a far cry from asking, within the presuppositions of the theological circle, whether and how faith can be made intelligible or attain to understanding in terms of congenial ontological reason. On the contrary, the issue now concerns the rationality of religious belief, often for those who do not participate in any religious tradition, judged in accordance with an ideal of rationality developed to accord with the sciences and common sense.

As will become clear, the rationality which is in question has little or nothing to do with the understanding and confirming of a faith already existent for a person within the theological circle; on the contrary, the supposition is that the inquirer is someone who is either outside the circle or on neutral ground, and his question is whether religious belief—taken in some generic sense—is sufficiently rational in character to propel him, so to speak, into some sort of religious commitment. Unless this is the aim of the inquirer, it would seem that the question of rationality is an idle one, and yet, as we shall see, the polarity of religion and the modern conception of rationality spawns the paradox that, although religious belief could not possibly be rational according to that standard, such belief, so it is thought, can and should be held on some other grounds—ultimacy, urgency, and perhaps even its very irrationality.

In the end, I have numerous questions and doubts about the adequacy and even the legitimacy of this entire procedure, but I purposely postpone expressing them at this point in the interest of facing directly and candidly the situation in which we actually find ourselves. In order to make clearer just what this situation is as regards resolving the problem of rationality in religion, I wish to consider the position outlined, albeit in fragmentary form, by Wittgenstein. He presents us with the most appropriate and consistent solution possible for someone whose approach to the problem is thoroughly conditioned by the polarity just described. In choosing this example, I am concerned not to be misunderstood. My purpose is not polemical, and I have no intention of taking advantage of the scattered and disjointed form in which Wittgenstein's views about religion and religious belief are available to us. The main drift of his thinking on the topic is fairly clear; my aim is to take his fideistic position as an illustration of what one is forced to conclude if he approaches the problem by taking some paradigm example of religious belief and then asking whether it is "rational" in accordance with a conception of rationality derivative from science and common sense. I should add that a similar, though by no means identical, account could be given if one were to choose Kierkegaard's position as a model, but it seems to me that our present situation is better illuminated by the response of an "outsider," so to speak. Kierkegaard was clearly speaking from within the Christian faith and tradition, whereas I believe it would be generally admitted that Wittgenstein was not and therefore that his thought furnishes us with a better illustration for our purposes. Let it be understood that I am making no personal judgments; Wittgenstein may have been more of an "insider" than Kierkegaard for that matter, but in his discussion of our topic it does not appear that he was speaking as a Christian theologian. He represents instead the modern secular thinker approaching the question of the nature and rationality of religious belief in accordance with the conception of rationality which has been dominant in Western thought since the eighteenth century.

On the basis of his lectures and conversations,[3] Wittgenstein was attempting to answer the question as to whether it is reasonable or unreasonable for a person to participate in religious belief. In order to do so, it was necessary for him to give some account of what is to be meant by 'religious belief'. Following the method of the paradigm case, Wittgenstein chose belief in a Last Judgment as his model[4] of a belief which is to be regarded without question as "religious." I shall simply follow the discussion without making an issue of Wittgenstein's identification of religion with religious belief, because despite my own belief that a simple identification of the two is not legitimate, I do not think that there can be any religious faith which totally excludes belief.

Wittgenstein's first point is that there is a great gulf between religious believers and nonbelievers which has no identifiable counterpart in cases of science and common sense. The claim is that if Mr. A. believes in a Last Judgment and Mr. B. says, "Possibly, I am not sure," the two are "poles apart"; whereas if Mr. A. says, "The airplane now taking off is a 747" and Mr. B. says, "You may be right, but I am not sure," the two are, according to Wittgenstein, "fairly near" in their views. From this it would appear that religion is an all or nothing affair and thus is set off from both science and common sense by a gulf which cannot be bridged.

The next point is that the enormous difference between believer and nonbeliever is "not simply" that the former thinks the evidence for a Last Judgment is well established, while the latter does not, because, according to Wittgenstein, someone could believe that there is evidence pointing to the occurrence of a Last Judgment in, say, 2,000 years, *without this being a religious belief*. On the other hand, says Wittgenstein, the believer could see that evidence for a Last Judgment is not nearly as firm as the evidence for believing in, for example, the existence of Napoleon, and yet the religious belief is for him "the firmest of all beliefs." Here we have a further indication of the disconnection between the religious context and those situations from which the ideal of rationality has been derived. According to the above example, one of the distinctive features of a "religious" belief is the absolute "firmness" with which it is believed. Possibilities and maybes are permissible in relation to all other kinds of belief, but if either pertains to a given belief it is *ipso facto* disqualified as religious.

Thus far Wittgenstein has been characterizing religious belief in largely external terms; he gives a more direct description when he tells us that religious belief is "guidance for this life." A person, he says, who believes in the Last Judgment has it always before his mind as an *unshakeable* belief and its status as such is manifest neither through reasoning nor appeal to ordinary grounds for beliefs but by its regulating all things in his life. Although the exact nature of this "regulating" is not spelled out, what Wittgenstein means is fairly clear. A person has a picture of a Last Judgment, a sort of ultimate or final accounting of life and its quality; he appeals to this picture in, for example foregoing pleasures, and he "risks things on account of it which he would not do on things which are by far better established for him."[5] The regulating in question, it would appear, is the hallmark of religious belief and is somehow the evidence, not for the belief itself, but for the fact that it is actually held as unshakeable. Emphasis falls less on the content of the belief itself and more on the belief in action, in the sense of its being responsible for what some believer does.

Not surprisingly, Wittgenstein concludes that belief in the case of religion means something entirely different from what it means in other contexts. In religion we have an "extraordinary" use of the word "believe," and hence there is an unbridgeable logical gap between that use and the use of the same term in "ordinary" situations which presumably means in scientific inquiry and common sense. How great the gap is can be seen from Wittgenstein's further claim that if the evidence for religious belief were such as would carry weight in science or history, or even sufficient to make the belief "indubitable," it would be insufficient in the religious context. The reason is, of course, that to speak of indubitability in what purports to be a cognitive context is totally to misunderstand what religious belief is about. Even an alleged indubitability would be irrelevant because, in Wittgenstein's own words, "the indubitability wouldn't be enough to make me change my whole life."[6]

It would, I think, be difficult to find a neater and more explicit illustration of the polarity between religion and the modern conception of rationality. In accordance with that conception which defines what we know and establishes the domain of the "ordinary," religion stands at the opposite pole as "extraordinary" and devoid of rationality. Religion has a regulating function with respect to a form of life, but the presumed ultimacy and unshakeability[7] of religious belief excludes it from the "more-or-less" factor which characterizes "ordinary" belief. Against this background, it is both understandable and consistent that Wittgenstein should answer in the negative his own question as to whether participation in religious belief is reasonable.

His treatment of the question, though brief, is most illuminating in pointing up the fideism which is the inevitable result of adopting a standard of rationality which is so narrow that it must exclude not only religion, but philosophy as well. For, as I shall point out, there are numerous philosophical assertions in Wittgenstein's own writings, including a statement specifying the standard of rationality itself, which are not certified either from the standpoint of any specific science or of common sense. There are people, says Wittgenstein, who base enormous things on evidence which, "taken in one way," is exceedingly weak. I assume that he is here thinking of the Last Judgment paradigm, the evidence for which, judged in accordance with so-called ordinary belief, is "weak," but people nevertheless regulate life by means of this belief. It is incorrect, he claims, to call these people unreasonable, but, he continues, "they are certainly not reasonable, that's obvious." Paradox at the least and contradiction at the most are both avoided by the claim that the matter is not one of reasonability at all. Wittgenstein can say that religious belief is not reasonable on the ground that it does not pretend to be, and like Kierkegaard, he bases this view on certain biblical passages which assert that not only is the basic New Testament faith not reasonable, but that it is in fact folly.[8] That this position does find expression in the canonical literature no student of the Bible can deny, but that fact does not prevent the dialectical philosopher from pointing out that the "folly" in question is not "sheer" folly, since the judgment that religious belief has this status is possible only on the assumption that there is a standard of rationality to which it is compared, and, further, that this standard is itself known to be the logical antithesis of folly. We shall return to this point later on; for the moment let it suffice to note that, as Hegel saw so well, there is a dialectical snag in every assertion of explicit irrationality which no philospher can escape, even if commonsensical minds are unaware of its existence.

Forcing religious belief to dwell entirely outside of the realm of rationality, as Wittgenstein does, has two decisive consequences each of which raises further problems by no means easy to resolve. In the first place, all "apologetics" is excluded, both "for" and "against" religious belief, because the enterprise itself implies that some religious belief is "true" and this automatically turns it into a "scientific hypothesis" with foundations so weak that the belief becomes "superstition." Not unlike the moralism displayed by Kierkegaard and Sartre, Wittgenstein's view subtly insinuates the existence of an inner insincerity on the part of those who seek for "reasons" in support of religious belief. The great tradition of "apologetics," which meant, not "apologizing" in embarrassment for an insecure position, but rather answering the questions about one's position advanced by critics, is entirely nullified. No rational forum for discussion exists; faith becomes a super paradox wherein paradox itself is seen not as a problem but rather as the solution to all problems.

Second, on Wittgenstein's view, the opponents of religious belief enjoy a position no more secure than that of believers; religious belief cannot be refuted on the grounds of insufficient evidence because "evidence" in this case is inappropriate. The "blunders" involved in religious belief are said to be too big simply to be dismissed as bad science. Once again religious belief and the standard of rationality are simply incommensurable. Here one is reminded of the witty comparison between religion and science once made by Chesterton: Science, he said, tells us a great many little truths in the interest of a great lie, whereas religion tells us a great many little lies in the interest of a great truth! But if the disparity between the two is absolute, nothing is to be learned from comparisons which are, in the end, quite illegitimate; no one could be said to know that religious belief is folly merely on the grounds that it is neither mathematics nor physics.

Thus far, I have been trying to show, taking Wittgenstein's general outlook as itself a paradigm, that a total fideism in religion is the position to which one is necessarily driven when rationality is defined exclusively in terms of science and common sense. Since there is no reality or dimension of reality about which or in relation to which religious belief could be true or valid, the only alternative is to construe it as performing some regulative function either with regard to some form or style of life taken in a comprehensive sense, or with regard to imperatives or commands offering guidance for action in specific situations where basically moral issues are involved. Driven from the temple of truth, religion must be content to exercise whatever sovereignty it can in the courtyard of practical reason. We come here to an absolutely crucial point. The emphasis on the practical is itself essential, but quite literally everything depends upon whether this practical dimension or function is part of a larger complex of thought and feeling based on some belief about the nature of things, or whether the practical function is *to take the place of* such a belief when the prevailing climate of opinion allows it no status above that of superstition. There can be no religion worthy of the name which does not include an ultimate commitment on the part of a person to a total life pattern informed by some vision, some image of the ground and goal of existence. In addition, there can be no religion worthy of the name which is devoid of ethical imperatives and principles governing the proper relations between man and man. But there is no way in which either the distinctively religious or moral dimension of life can be sustained by actual beings in the absence of some convictions about the nature of man, the universe and its ground which are held to be true or valid and thus expressive of the reality we confront.

The point can be seen from Wittgenstein's own example of a Last Judgment. It does no good to say that a person has this belief always before him in unshakeable form regulating for all his life, unless there is some difference between the belief itself and the regulating function. That is to say, the belief means that there *is* a judge, a *persona*, an all-encompassing center of knowledge capable of making the judgment, and I fail to see how the belief could perform its function of guidance in the life of the individual unless he or she believed in the reality of that judge. Whatever the regulating function is and means, it cannot take the place of the belief itself. The person does not believe in the regulating function but rather in the reality of the judge, although he is certainly committed to the guidance offered by the belief at every point. The main reason for the inadequacy of all the practicalistic and fideistic solutions to the dilemma of religious knowledge since Kant is found in their tendency to *identify* the belief content with the function it has to perform and thus to evade the issue of what validity is to be attached to the belief itself. Or if this issue is raised, it is most likely to be resolved by an appeal to postulates, if not to fictions, and the exhortation to act "as if" some belief were true.

At this point it may be objected that criticism of proposed solutions does not of itself suffice to resolve the main problem. I entirely agree, but it seems to me important nevertheless to understand the full force of the situation we are in at the present time. If I am correct in thinking that Wittgenstein's position is representative of much current philosophical thinking about our topic, then we face the unhappy dilemma that on the one hand religious belief cannot be permeated by rationality in any way and, on the other, if it could, it would *ipso facto* lose its religious character, becoming instead a low-grade form of science. This solution is incoherent because of the tortuous dichotomy it introduces into human life. We are not to suppose that the world is made up of two distinct kinds of individuals— men of science and men of faith, each dwelling in a separate sphere. There is simply man confronting himself, other persons, the world, and whatever other realities there may be, and life in that world requires *both* knowledge about it and some resolution of the problem to which religion speaks, namely who we are, why we are, and what the whole thing means. In short, there is only one man who must dwell *simultaneously* in the two dimensions which Wittgenstein's solution tears apart and leaves totally disconnected. The solution is unstable and can lead only to some form of schizophrenia.

Since in my view there can be no coherent philosophical resolution of the problem of rationality in religion without the questioning of cherished assumptions and a radical reorientation in thought, I can do no more than indicate what seems to me necessary in order to bring these changes about. The first step is to return to our basic situation, which is that of individual language-using beings who find themselves in the world experiencing, describing, attempting to explain what there is, and also seeking to interpret their life so as to take account of the value, the importance and the purpose that permeates it at every turn. The reason I find unsatisfactory the view which supposes that participation in religious belief of

some sort is a pure option to be decided on the basis of an estimate of its "rationality" is that the supposition runs counter
to experience. It belongs to man as man in the world to raise
the religious question of the ground and goal of his own existence, so that some form of religious concern is inescapable,
whether that concern is fulfilled through adherence to a recognizable religious tradition or to any number of current substitutes ranging from Marxism to Transcendental Meditation.
An important consequence of this fact is that it transforms
the entire question of rationality in religion. Instead of establishing some standard of rationality on the basis of science
and common sense, and then asking whether religious belief is
"rational" in that sense, we must attempt to make critical
comparisons between beliefs within the universe of discourse
established by the religions themselves and their secular coun-
terparts. Hegel set the pattern here in the very similar case of
philosphy when he demanded that rival philosophical views
should be set in a critical dialectic with each other for the purpose of determining their relative coherence, comprehensive-
ness, degree of illumination, and fidelity to experience. The
justification for this procedure is that the only legitimate
comparisions are those made between systems of discourse of *the
same logical type*, as distinct from an approach like that of
Kant where the assessment of metaphysical and theological
theses was made in accordance with cognitive conditions in no
way peculiar to these types of thought but derived instead from
physical science and mathematics.

We are brought to an acknowledgement of two essential
points; first, that all talk of rationality in religion is dependent
on the determination of the standard of rationality, as is quite
evident when one considers the high degree to which religious
faith was made intelligible through the ontological reason of an
Anselm and the extent to which it appears as unintelligible in
terms of the scientific reason of a Wittgenstein. In either case,
the standard of rationality is the crux, which brings us to the
second point. The specification of such a standard in any
historical epoch is an inescapably *philosophical* affair, which
must be argued in philosophical terms; it can never be a matter

simply of science or comon sense. Notice, however, that in the long development of empiricist conceptions of knowledge and rationality—including, for example, the claim of Russell that "What science cannot discover, mankind cannot know," the empiricist criterion of meaning, and even Wittgenstein's ordinary rationality—*philosophy itself ceases to be a form of knowledge* and becomes instead either a hermeneutic device for clarifying what other people say or a neutral liaison between branches of inquiry which do have cognitive status. If philosophy is excluded from the precinct of knowledge, then the assertion of a standard of rationality for judging religious or any other kind of belief can be no more than a stipulation, a convention, or a dogmatic claim which is not made the less dogmatic by finding support in majority opinion. But this is not all; the loss of faith in a philosophical reflection having cognitive reach goes hand in hand with the exclusion of religious belief from the sphere of rationality. This is not because the two are the same, but because they are akin. The long tradition of treating religious ideas and beliefs in philosophical fashion is more than an historical accident. The two enterprises are essentially connected and the fate of one must have repercussions for that of the other.

I cannot here attempt to repeat what I have written on other occasions about the need for religion to have an appropriate framework for expression. For centuries it was metaphysics and speculative philosophy. With their decline, other frameworks have been forthcoming; religion, it was thought, might be expressed as morality, as the realm of value, as history, as poetry, as play, as performative utterance and, under the aegis of linguistic philosphy, as language itself. And more recently we are told that sociology and psychology are the most appropriate channels for the expression of religious belief. In every case, these frameworks or theological firmaments, as I like to call them, were regarded as substitutes for, or successors to, the classical ontological frameworks which had so long served as the intelligible medium of expression for religious belief. While I have no intention whatever of denying the contribution to be made by all these media for clarifying, interpreting, and helping to make meaningful past religious beliefs, I do not see how any of them in the end can avoid coming to terms with the ontological dimension and the sort of reality to which religious insight points.

Against the background of the modern climate of opinion, I can envisage but one avenue of approach whereby a form of rationality and intelligibility can be recovered within the sphere of religious belief and that is through a revised and strengthened form of the ancient enterprise which went by the name of 'faith seeking understanding.' Starting with the assumption that it is hopeless to deal with the question of rationality in religion by invoking a standard which excludes the possibility of such rationality in advance, this approach seeks to find a rationality appropriate to, and commensurate with, the nature of religious belief. The measure of this appropriateness is found in the similarity between the ontological dimension represented by philosophy and the religious dimension represented by theology. Both construe reality in ultimate and comprehensive, or holistic, forms and this is their point of contact. The attempt, however, to attain to an understanding of faith under contemporary conditions will fail if it amounts to no more than a repetition of the past. At least three significant changes are necessary. First, the connotations of utter changelessness and timelessness which were attached to the traditional conception of Being as the ultimate category must give way to the concepts of life and spirit implying not only change and development but also relationality with a world of time and history. Secondly, reason can no longer be conceived as the timeless surveyor of fixed forms, but must be understood instead as a living power of understanding and intelligibility operating within the streams of experience which constitute the lives of individual persons. Finally, experience—as that significant and purposeful deposit resulting from the interaction between a sign-using animal and the reality it confronts—must be accorded the objective status it deserves so that it can function as a reliable medium for understanding the religious belief which is an interpretation of that experience. It is highly significant that in recent decades the only philosophical positions that have been able to sustain any rational dialogue with religious belief—the philosophy of process and organism, the several forms of existentialism, and American pragmatism—have all been the constructive, not the critical, positions, and each gives evidence of wanting to emphasize the three changes in outlook I have just mentioned. Without the recovery of a constructive philosophy along these lines which would make possible a new version of the enterprise known as "faith seeking understanding," the task of finding any rationality or intelligibility in religious belief seems to me frankly hopeless.

It may indeed come as a disappointment that I am unable to offer any solution to our main problem other than a program to be worked out. But that is the way our contemporary situation appears to me, especially in the light of my own efforts to generate philosophico-religious dialogue over the past thirty years. Perhaps it may not be out of order to close with an anecdote which throws light on what needs to be done. A number of years ago, I participated in what was then called a Don's Conference at Oxford, bringing together philosophers and religious thinkers for discussion about the nature and meaning of religious belief. For several sessions I was quite frankly impressed by the high degree of communication that took place and the seriousness of the attempts being made to understand religious ideas and insight in their own terms. This initial success was due in part to the influence of the then novel viewpoint, sometimes associated with Wittgenstein, that the important consideration in dealing with any type of language is not the meaning but the use. The harmony of this conference, however, was to be severely jolted when Ian Ramsey, who was to give a major address, chose as his subject a treatment, in terms of his theory of logical mapping and religious grammar, of the post-resurrection appearances of Jesus as expressed in biblical language. I must confess that, upon taking note of this topic on the program beforehand, I could not avoid the feeling that he was pressing his luck! And indeed, I turned out to be right, but the important point is the reason why. He had barely finished when the empiricist meaning criterion, which until this time had been in abeyance and uninvoked, made its appearance with a vengeance. What, it was asked, is the *ordinary* meaning of the term 'resurrection'? And the theologians present, instead of insisting that the question falls in the same category with the equally fruitless one of asking what is the *ordinary* meaning of the term 'laser beam', began to look for this ordinary meaning. The result was chaos and no intelligibility. The reason is simple, the tools at hand were inadequate for the job. Neither common sense nor science will suffice for dealing with the elaborate concepts which belong to an integrated system of theological interpretation. Since, as it seems to me, the type of meaning expressed in religion is closer to that of philosophy than to either science or common sense, the recovery of a constructive philosophy as a medium for understanding and interpreting religious belief is what is most needed. This does not mean that science and ordinary experience are excluded as of no account; a living religious tradition must in the end become moribund if it isolates itself from the development of scientific knowledge and from the cultural patterns which structure the daily life of a people.

As regards the last point, the need for religion to be related to the findings of science and their implications, it is important to take note of a development in recent decades that seems to me to carry with it the greatest promise for a new understanding of the relations between science, philosophy, and religion. I refer to the enterprise of the history of science and to the new philosophical perspectives that have come about as a result of taking that history seriously. For too long it had been assumed that science—usually identified with physics—represents a steady, cumulative advance of knowledge, accompanied by universal agreement concerning both basic facts and their proper explanation. Attention to the facts of actual inquiry and the historical conditions under which it takes place has served not only to correct this oversimplified picture but to bring about a reappraisal of the reigning hypothetical-deductive model of scientific explanation as well. There is today a new appreciation for the meaning of scientific inquiry *in situ*, that it is conducted by what Peirce called a "flesh and blood experimenter" working in historical context, that there is a greater difference of opinion between orthodox and heterodox interpretations than was previously acknowledged, and, finally, that science's involvement in technology has led to its own industrialization and to the introduction of limiting conditions— economic, social, and ethical—which make it increasingly difficult to draw a neat distinction between "pure" and "applied" science.

Before proceeding, a note of caution is in order. I do not share the view of those who regard the new understanding of science as grounds for the "subjectivizing" of scientific knowledge and even for its dissolution into "ideology" or purely relativistic perspectives. On the contrary, the disclosure of a more complete picture of the develoment of scientific inquiry leads not to a less but to a greater objectivity concerning the sort of knowledge which has transformed our lives and revolutionized our way of looking at the world.

A second result of the new historical approach is a new perspective on the relations between science and philosophy. The questioning of the simple, automatic progress conception of scientific development shows that the sciences are less "pure" than was previously believed; on many scientific issues there are differing "schools" of thought, not to be harmonized by appeal to so-called "crucial" experiments. These differences are as much the result of divergent philosophical assumptions as of other factors in the situation of scientific inquiry. The important point is the need to revise the old and much used contrast between philosophy and science, forcefully stated by Kant, according to which philosophical knowledge is suspect because there are within it schools of thought, indicating a lack of consensus which impedes progress, while true science is all consensus and marked by continual, linear progress. There are now grounds for reconsidering the large gap which has opened up between science and philosophy; a more accurate picture suggests that science is not the neat and finished affair previously assumed and that philosophy, by comparison, is not the chaotic confusion of tongues which it has been taken to be, especially by those who adopt highly developed sciences as the one model for all knowing.

Study of the history of science has had the salutary effect of calling attention both to the existence and the inescapability of rational or interpretative frameworks in every field of intellectual endeavor. No one simply collects facts, projects philosophical ideas, or reports the primary experiences from which religion draws its inspiration. Without the conceptual frameworks represented by scientific theories, by the categorial schemes of metaphysics, and by the concepts and doctrines of theology, it is impossible for us to deal adequately with the experience of the world and ourselves which forms the basis of all thinking and knowing. The presence of an identical element in science, philosophy, and religion in the form of these frameworks should allow for an increased understanding and communication between the three modes of thought and experience.

The truth disclosed by science does not confront the insights of religion directly and immediately, except in rare cases where some religious belief can confidently be regarded as contradicted by well-attested scientific evidence. The *implications* of scientific knowledge are what count, and these need first to be developed—as, for example, in the case of the theory of evolution—in order to see what bearing they have upon religious doctrine. Philosophy and theology as reflective disciplines are necessary for determining these implications and their further consequences for the content of faith. These two disciplines must perform a mediating function between scientific truth and religion in its primary experiences and insights. Whitehead stated the point very well in *Religion in the Making*; the fact that he emphasized "metaphysics" rather than theology need not cause a problem, because all self-critical theologians in the Western tradition have been aware of their involvement in metaphysical assumptions. "Religion," he wrote, "requires a metaphysical backing; for its authority is endangered by the intensity of the emotions which it generates. Such emotions are evidence of some vivid experience; but they are a very poor guarantee for its correct interpretation."[9]

NOTES

1. Anselm, it is true, was at times more ambitious in his aims and claims, proposing to demonstrate religious truths to "outsiders" who did not share his premises.

2. Even Peirce, who was the staunchest defender of the irreducibility of the conceptual order, at times objected to identifying religion as "belief," on the ground that belief implies a distance between the person and the object of belief which is inappropriate and distorts the nature of religion as a lived affair.

3. Wittgenstein, *Lectures and Conversations on Aesthetics, Psychology and Religious Belief*, compiled from notes taken by Y. Smythies, et al., ed. Cyril Barret (Berkeley and Los Angeles, 1967). See also the commentary by W. D. Hudson, "Some Remarks on Wittgenstein's Account of Religious Belief," in *Talk of God*, Royal Institute of Philosophy Lectures, Vol. 2, 1967–68 (London, 1969).

4. The matter cannot be discussed here, but it is curious in the extreme that Wittgenstein and others sympathetic to his mode of thought invariably approach the subject of religion, not by attending to its roots in human experience and its role in human life, but by selecting some doctrine, such as life after death or the paradigm example used in the test, which is "eschatological," heavily dependent on the religious imagination and theological elaboration and hence not readily connectible with either reason or experience. It is as if one were to approach the task of persuading a skeptical person of the value of philosophy by proposing that he first master Kant's transcendental deduction or Whitehead's method of extensive abstraction.

5. Wittgenstein, *Lectures*, p. 54.

6. Wittgenstein, *Lectures*, p. 57.

7. It is important to notice that the "unshakeability" in question has nothing to do with the logical status of a belief, but only with the absolute tenacity with which it is held by the believer.

8. In 1 Cor. 1:23. The Christian preaching of the crucified Christ is said to be "foolishness" ($\mu\alpha\rho\iota\varkappa$) to the Greeks among whom it is understood or judged in accordance with worldly wisdom. The contrast between divine and human wisdom was one of the favorite paradoxes of St. Paul.

9. A. N. Whitehead, *Religion in the Making* (New York, 1926), p. 83.

The Dialectic of Christian Belief: Rational, Incredible, Credible

LANGDON GILKEY

It is hardly original, though it is ironic, to point out the complexity, not to say the murkiness, of our subject—rationality and Christian belief. How intellectual clarity is related to religious conviction is itself unclear; how the mystery of faith is qualified by rationality is itself mysterious. Our purpose in this paper, therefore, is not to provide a finished answer to this question; rather as a beginning it is to uncover some of the more important issues involved and so some of the reasons this question is itself a part of the mystery of faith. I will speak about the rationality of Christian belief instead of that of religious belief in general. The relation of rationality to religious belief takes an entirely different form in other religious traditions than our own (for example in Buddhism). Our discussion will be useful only if it deals with its subject concretely, in relation to the issue for rationality that the particular form of Christianity poses.

At the start it may be helpful to point out two importantly different ways the question of rationality and Christian belief arises. These two forms of the question are quite distinct from each other and yet these two distinct modes intertwine in each phase of every discussion of this theme and can, unless held distinct in the mind, breed all sorts of confusion. First there is the relation of what can possibly be proved in the corpus of Christian faith (e.g., the theistic claim) to other aspects of the faith which cannot be proved (e.g., the incarnation, atonement, etc.). If the question is posed thusly, i.e., as a relation between what is provable and what may be credible on other grounds, then rationality includes the first, provable part, and Christian belief appears as referent to that rational part *plus* all the other symbols that cannot be proved—and our question concerns the relation of these two parts to each other, a question investigated with great power by St. Thomas. The question, however, of rationality and Christian belief may refer to another relation entirely, namely that between Christianity as a total system of beliefs, Christianity as a possibility on the one hand, and Christianity as a qualification of our existence, as reflection qualifying not ideas so much as life on the other hand. This distinction between the aesthetic system and the integration or reduplication of the system (as rational, irrational, or credible) into human existence and praxis was made crystal clear by Kierkegaard. Obviously, in this Kierkegaardian context the relation of rationality to Christian belief changes its referents: rationality now referring to the total corpus as a rational or aesthetic possibility subject to direct argument, and Christian belief (faith) referring to Christian reflection as it qualifies our existence, and thus a mode of reflection not at all subject to direct argument.

I would suggest that much of the confusion associated with this problem has arisen from failing to keep these two sets of distinctions themselves distinct. Thus, for example, many have heatedly denied the possibility of a natural theology because they were conscious of the second distinction, namely that between the requirements of rational possibility and those of religious existence; or, alternatively, many have defended the role of rational argument and of coherent system by denying as irrelevant the existential element—the element of decision and commitment—to Christian reflection. On the whole, except for the last part of this paper, we shall stay within the confines of the first context, namely that which considers Christianity as an aesthetic possibility for reflection, debate, and direct argument, a *possibility* for decision, and not within the context which considers how Christianity becomes or might become a qualification of our existence. In this specified context we shall ask about the various complex issues in the relation of rationality to Christian belief.

The general issue we shall explore concerns the relation of what may be called the rationality in Christian belief to the other elements which may be believed but are not provable by reason alone—St. Thomas' issue as noted above. I will use the word 'credible' for those other elements to indicate that although they cannot be proved by reason from general experience, they are not irrational and can in fact be defended and/or warranted by various forms of relevant argument. My main thesis is that there is a dialectic in the relation of rationality and Christian belief, a dialectic which moves from rationality through incredibility to credibility. If this be so, then the rational and the credible elements of Christian faith, while distinct in their grounds and their warrants, nevertheless are dialectically interdependent such that the rationality of the one and the credibility of the other disappears if either element is separated or isolated from the other. The same point can be put in another way: Christianity is credible only as a total system of symbols. While some of its essential symbols may be demonstrable in isolation, nevertheless, if they are left in isolation, they forfeit their rationality and become incredible and so *a fortiori* irrational. Thus while a natural theology is an integral and essential moment in the total dialectic of Christian belief, it is a part within a wider, credible whole, an aspect of the total viewpoint of faith. Its rationality, while defensible and significant, is therfore itself in the end dependent on the more elusive, less rigorous, and scarcely "natural" intelligibility and meaning characteristic of the faith as a whole. Let us now seek to make clear this thesis and to disclose its grounds, its dialectic, and the interdependence of moments within it.

I

Among the many areas where this thesis may be illustrated, the historical character of our being, both individual and social, is one of the most useful. For Christianity in its scriptures and

in most, if not all, of its theological formulations concerns itself
with both the structure and the meaning of our historical being,
and obviously many of our own deepest existential and religious
issues arise in relation to our historicity. Finally, and not
insignificantly to my proposal, I have pondered the relation
of Christianity to historicity for some time. Now our own
question enters because when one analyzes the synchronic
structure of our temporal being, a number of (to me) convincing
arguments appear for positing a divine ground and context for
that being. Thus does the theistic claim arise and does Christianity receive its essential component of "rationality," the
natural theological base for all else that is affirmed. On the
other hand, the human experience of the diachronic character of
its historical being, either as an individual or as a member of a
historical group, has indicated—as often as not—that that historical being is alienated and estranged, immersed in a destiny that is
chaotic, incoherent, and grimly determined or fated for suffering,
and faced with possibilities that are menacing and destructive
as much as they are creative. The structure of our historical
being leads to the claim that temporal finitude has its source
in a divine creative ground; yet the character of our concrete
historical existence as estranged and alienated can continually
obscure that divine ground in conflict, meaninglessness, suffering, and despair. The result is that at that point *deus* becomes
radically *absconditus*, and the theistic claim begins now to
seem incredible and the arguments that ground it irrational.
The concrete reality of historical being as both temporal and
estranged now challenges the rationality and meaningfulness
of finite existence, the sense of the reality of God, and as a consequence the rationality of religious or of Christian belief.
Ironically, however, it is also precisely at that point that the
deeper relevance of the theistic claim appears for the first time,
and the real significance of the divine ground—and of belief—
enter. For in relation to our estrangement the divine, obscured
now as ground, manifests itself as redemptive. This redemptive
movement, as we would all surely agree, represents both the
center of Christian witness and the basis of whatever ultimate
importance Christian belief may have. Finally, this redemptive

presence of the divine in grace—in new insight and new life—is by the nature of the case not "rational" in the above sense. It is not present in the analyzable essential structure of historical being. It is given to it in answer to the warping and self-destruction of that structure. It is at best credible, not "rational"—but without that credibility based on redemptive grace, the rationality of theism which is its foundation is itself subverted, just as without the rational foundation with which we began, the credibility of the articles of grace is dissolved.

A dialectic essential to the character of Christian belief has appeared that has had confusing reverberations all through the history of Christian reflection. Catholicism has clearly recognized these two separable but interrelated moments, but—to my mind—integrated them wrongly in terms of the two levels of nature and of grace, a structure almost inconceivable to the modern historical consciousness. Protestantism rightly challenged that structure but tended itself to overlook the dialectic. The result hs been that it either took the second and third moments as decisive, i.e., estrangement, incredibility, and kerygma, or it took only the first as decisive, natural theology and a "natural" grace. In a way, of course, both traditions are right and yet both also wrong.

Seemingly, if we would establish the legitimacy—the rationality—of the theistic underpinning of a Christian interpretation of life, we must emphasize historical being's ontological structure as good, intelligible, and meaningful and through that structure the relation to a divine ground, i.e., a philosophical theism. But, by the same token and almost by necessity, such an emphasis on the first moment's possibility overlooks, as subversive of that rationality, history's self-contradiction and tragedy, its warping and obscuring of that structure, and its overwhelming need of grace. If, on the other hand, we would proclaim the relevance and legitimacy of the redemptive side of a Christian interpretation of life, we must emphasize the contradictions apparent in history's actuality and the incredibility of grace, and so obscure the reality and intelligibility of the God who purports to redeem. A natural theology seems to miss—or be in danger of doing so—the actual or concrete

character of history's life and to make irrelevant the message
of the redemption it seeks rationally to defend. A purely keryg-
matic Christianity, aware of evil and centered in the surprising
gift of grace, seems either to undermine its own ontological
and theological foundations or else to assert at the end an
ultimate coherence and rationality it so vigorously denied at
its inception.

The dialectical interdependence—our initial thesis—of the
rational and the credible parts of the Christian corpus is here
illustrated. On the one hand, no redemptive possibilities are
fully rational or even credible unless their grounds are rationally
coherent with the essential structure of our being; on the other
hand, concrete existence makes the very rationality of theism
incredible unless the reality of redemptive grace is found in
some way credible. This is, I suspect, the reason that the arguments of natural theology, its component of rationality, appear
to be rational only to those who also find the remainder of
Christian affirmation credible.

Christian belief is based rationally on a philosophical
analysis of our finitude; but that very rationality is itself dependent, granted the estrangement of the actuality of our
existence and the consequent hiddenness of God, on the
credibility of the other elements of Christian belief which
cannot be so demonstrated. There is a dialectic of rationality,
incredibility, and credibility that constitutes the formal
structure of Christian belief, with the negative, estrangement,
initiating the movement from one moment to the other. If
these moments are separated, each one loses its status, and
Christianity dissolves as a total interpretation of life. If they
are not distinguished, then untold confusion results. If they
are held in distinction and yet tension, then rationality and
credibility join to make intelligible the incredible grace and
promise which Christian faith proclaims.

II

In order to explore this dialectic of rationality, incredibility,
and credibility further, let us look more closely at the character

of historical being in order to see the initial rationality of theism, the effects of estrangement on that rationality, and the final moment of what may be called the credibility of an incredible grace.

An ontological analysis of our finitude reveals, I believe, that finitude is most basically to be characterized as temporal or in process, and that the structure of that process is one of destiny—a given from our immediate past and that of our world—in union with freedom or self-actualization. Such an ontological structure can be shown to be the presupposition of our experience of ourselves and of the history in which we are immersed, of social and political life, and finally of those who study history and seek to understand it—be they historicans, social scientists, futurologists, or philosophers, and however much they may deny the presence of such ontological presuppositions or scorn inquiry into them. Now the point is that while this ontological structure makes possible the openness, the contingency, and the "fallenness" of history —and thus opens the door to history's disorder, irrationality, and meaninglessness, as well as to its creativity—nevertheless it itself entails a deeper, necessary, all-encompassing ground as the condition of its possibility. This entailment is present in all three phases of temporal passage: the relation of past destiny to present, the self-actualization of the present out of that destiny and novel possibility, and the relation of future possibility to present. We cannot here give more than an outline of these arguments; intimations of one or another of them are to be found in Augustine, Thomas, Calvin, Schleiermacher, Tillich, and especially Whitehead.

If finite being be temporal, in process, then it is characterized by radical passingness, the vanishing of what has just become, the relative non-being of what has been actual. This characteristic of temporal being, that the past fades and only the present is real, makes possible both creative freedom and the new; its shadow side is the loss of the immediate past, its disappearance into relative unreality and so ineffectiveness. But one of the mysteries of time is that the achieved past is nevertheless effective. It forms the destiny for each present, providing it with its continuing reality, shaping in part its form, and thus making possible "substances" or enduring entities, causality, experience and cognition. All relations, continuity, order, and thus all life itself depend on the effectiveness in the arising present of a past which, if being be temporal, has vanished into relative non-being. Thus entailed in the relation of the past that is gone to a present made and made itself by that past is the presence of a deeper, creative ground, a ground that does not pass away but brings each achieved and objectified past into the creative present as the latter's formative destiny, its initial data, the origin of its thrownness and its facticity. The ground of the contingent, self-actualizing present, and so of all secondary causality and cognition, is, as Augustine and Thomas both said, a primary causality that is not contingent but necessary, or as Whitehead terms it, a creativity out of which new occasions arise. This is what the classical tradition in theology has called the first work of providence, "the preservation of the creature over time." Such a timeless divine work in time is directly entailed by the radical temporality of all creaturely being.

The past forms in large part the present—but never completely. In history, however much all seems determined by destiny, there is always a response that is creative of the actual event. Thus does freedom, the principle of self-actualization, enter the historical process; each occasion is in part *causa sui*, else all be determined and novelty be as unreal as would be intentions, decisions, errors, and sin. If this be so, then another "mystery" in the midst of passage has appeared, namely the deeper ground of freedom itself. For *ipso facto* the power to be and to be free cannot arise either from the past or even from given possibility—else there be no *self-actualization*. And as Schleiermacher points out, our experience of freedom is not an experience of originating our freedom. As Augustine and Thomas reiterate, the power of all secondary causality is a *given*, not a self-created, power— and by its nature not given by any creaturely reality behind or ahead of us. Thus again there is entailed in the character of passage, this time in that of the self-actualizing present, a deeper, necessary, creative divine ground from which each occasion as self-formative arises; this is the second, "concurring" work of providence whereby freedom comes to be in each historical event.

Finally, there is no temporal event without the impingement on it of future and so of novel possibility—as Whitehead, Bloch, and the eschatologists have reminded us. Not only novelty but also openness, genuine alternatives, and so freedom, depend on this effective presence of real possibility to each self-actualizing present. But, as Whitehead has shown, possibilities to be and to be effective "must be somewhere," related to actuality, for only actuality can provide an effective reason for anything actual. And in a world characterized by self-actualizing freedom as well as open possibility, possibilities must be primordially graded into a relevant order if they are to help fashion an orderly actuality. Thus there must be a primordial actuality that includes in its envisionment all of possibility as possible, setting those novel forms into a relevant order and thus providing the ontological ground for novelty, openness, and freedom in experience. Novelty in the midst of continuing order characterizes our experience of temporal being; such experience is unintelligible without a divine ground, both of continuity and of freedom, and now of relevant possibility. This is the third and final ontological role of providence, as "directing" passage through its eternal envisionment of relevant possibilities for the changing flux.

In all three of its phases temporal being requires some ground beyond temporality and yet actively within it: as the continuing source of the destiny from the immediate past, as the ground of present self-actualization, and as the creative "place" of future possibility. Those aspects of the structure of temporal being that have originally seemed to challenge the rationality of theism: the non-being of time, the freedom of temporal being, and the unlimited openness of new possibilities, far from denying theism, require it rationally. Rationality is deeply characteristic of the most fundamental claim of Christian faith about the reality and effectiveness of God in historical passage.

III

The ontological structure of historical being, then, pro-claims the rationality of theism. It is, however, also true that the concrete character of historical actuality deeply challenges the rationality of that claim. For the actuality of historical existence is estranged from this structure of destiny, freedom, and creative possibility. Creative destiny, freedom, and open possibility appear, to be sure, in much historical experience, for such experience would not be possible without them; and many epochs of history—for example, the period of early modernity—experienced this meaningful and creative side of history as history's predominant character. Nevertheless, to other periods and to those groups and classes which are not dominant, historical passage manifests a different, grim-mer, and less creative face. At such times and for such groups, destiny is in union neither with freedom nor with possibility. Rather, the given from the historical past, embodied in warped institutions, chaotic events, and twisted characters, appears as Fate, as a given which crushes freedom and is void of genuine and creative possibility. Here the ontological structure of history is warped, fallen, or—in Tillich's word—estranged. This is an objective, though not necessitated, characteristic of historical being, not merely an inward, psychological, or existential quality. For the injustice of institutional forms is objective; historical conflicts are objective; and the disorder and suffering that result are no mere psychological matters, as surely the nemesis awaiting each warped civilization is as objective, and more concrete, than any economic graph. At such times, moreover, the ontological structure of history as destiny, freedom, and possibility is radically obscured. Destiny has become fate; freedom is bound within evil choices or arbitrary and ineffective spasms; and creative possibilities seem unreal. Obviously, at such times and from such a per-spective, the theistic claim, based on a structure that is estranged from itself and so now obscured, itself appears as ungrounded, irrational, and even oppressive. Heralding a destiny that is really fate, theism appears as an ideology blessing the dubious status quo; proclaiming a freedom that is in fact oppressed, it appears as unrealistic idealism; in promising possibilities that seem impossible, it seems delusory, an opiate. The estrangement of the structure of historical being makes incredible the rational implications of that essential structure. And because religion itself participates fully in that estrangement, its very rationality, persuasiveness, and promise can become demonic, themselves a part of the warped character of historical life—as most social revolutionaries have rightly felt. As we noted, in the face of the warped actuality of history, the rational component of faith, descriptive of the essential structure of passage but not of its fallen concreteness, becomes either a pious and ineffective abstraction or a demonic ideology, and so incredible to eyes fastened on the concreteness of history's actuality.

Profound theology has had much to say about the *deus absconditus*. The source of this negative symbol in the experiences of fatedness, meaninglessness, suffering, and judgment are evident. For the actuality of historical experience is filled with all of these, and it follows that the creative providence of God as we have described it is surely neither experienced nor known there. In these brief remarks on this theme I would like to dwell more on the basis in ontological structure of passage to this radical hiddenness—the incredibility of God —than on the phenomenological or ontic description of the estrangement of history. Any contemporary assessment of the social present and immediate prospects of our technological, nationalistic, and capitalistic society will fill in the latter.

The relation of ontological structure to its estrangement is, of course, exceedingly close. Because of the structure as freedom, the estrangement is possible; and because of the estrangement, the structure is obscured. This is the deepest ground, relevant at least to philosophical inquiry and so to "rationality," of what we have called the incredibility of theism— though, as noted, the qualitative, ontic character of a warped history in conflict, injustice, suffering, and meaninglessness also provides ample ground for an existential incredibility.

We have pictured the creative work of providence as providing that continuing unity of past, present, and future that
makes an event possible and that is, therefore, the ontological
condition for temporal being, being in process. Thus through
the work of God is non-being overcome and temporal finitude
emerges: achieved actuality is brought as creative destiny
into the present as the condition of the continuity of being
and of structure; self-actualization emerges as formative of
that destiny in the light of presented alternatives; and future
possibilities are present as novel and creative options to this
complex of past and present. When, however, the relation of
the emerging event to its divine ground is transformed in
estrangement, this creative structure, while not lost—else
temporal finitude cease to be—is warped. The unity of past,
present, and future created and upheld by providence is broken,
and historical actuality takes on that new character made
familiar by phenomenological analyses of sin, conflict, meaninglessness, and despair. Now the past is either lost, making
the present empty of reality, or it becomes an all-determining
fate that crushes the present and the future. With its divine
ground obscured, freedom loses touch with its own destiny,
and so with itself—and the present entity faces self-negation
or self-elevation. Overwhelmed by contingency or fatedness
in the given and in itself, freedom despairs of its role in self-
and in world-creation. And possibility, no longer related
creatively to destiny, appears as arbitrary, orderless, and unreal.
Sin results, ontologically and experientially, in the loss of
the unity of past, present, and future: the vanishing of the
past into unaccessible unreality, the smothering of the present
as determined by fate, and the closing of the future as bereft
of possibility.

In each phase of temporality, unreality and non-being—
and so suffering—dominate our individual and social existence.
Under such circumstances historical existence—and the individual lives immersed in it—appears as fated, meaningless,
and suffused with suffering and guilt; and philosophical
reflection finds only these as the essential character of what
it scrutinizes. Let us note that even the immanent ontological

structure of temporal finitude, as destiny, freedom, and possibility, is "absconditus." Thus *a fortiori* its divine ground disappears and "is silent." This is why in epochs dominated by a sense of estrangement rather than of essential structure a rationally "incredible" providence becomes, through faith, the only basis for confidence in that essential structure, in destiny, freedom, and possibility as foundational to all finite being—as the examples of Augustine and Calvin so clearly show. In any case, on the ontological as well as on the ontic descriptive level of analysis, the negative moment of the dialectic, estrangement, seems at this point to overwhelm the positive thesis constituting the rationality of theistic providence and to make the latter incredible. And let us further note, if this analysis be correct, that the more the *historical* or process character of finite being is emphasized, the more the effects of estrangement on the cognition of the divine ground, as well as on the power of the human will, will of necessity be emphasized—for it is only eternity that holds the moments of our time together, and a radically temporal process without the divine ground tends to fall apart.

If, as Barth says, it be Catholic to emphasize a natural theology, and if it be Protestant to emphasize the effects of sin on the possibility of the knowledge of God—though both assertions must be carefully qualified—we have in the pursuit of our theme uncovered a dialectical interpretation of *both* the Catholic and the Protestant moments. The structural foundation of Christian faith, the theistic claim that there is a divine ground to historical passage, can be rationally argued from the ontological structure of passage. However as we have just shown, both that structure and its ground become obscured by the concrete actuality of historical existence. In this situation not only does that rationality become irrational—or incredible—but by making it central to the statement of the faith, the concreteness of historical life can be overlooked, the deepest relevance of the gospel forgotten, and the faith turned into a pious abstraction unrelated to existential concreteness or, as noted, a dangerous ideology too much related to the divinely given. On the other hand, those further symbolic elements of the faith that describe, judge, and seek to resolve this estrangement through the witness to redemption, i.e., the law and the gospel, have no meaning and structure, and surely no intelligibility, without this original foundation. As Irenaeus and Tertullian argued against the gnostics, God cannot be judge and redeemer unless he is also creator of all and sovereign lord of historical passage; the gospel of redemption is scarcely credible without the rational foundation of theism. Thus are the two elements with which we began, the rational and the credible elements, interrelated because of the incredible but real moment of estrangement that intervenes and makes each in its own way in turn incredible. Estrangement makes a rational theism *rationally* incredible, as most of intellectual modernity avers; and it makes the appearance of redemption existentially incredible unexpected, and unmerited (the marks of the presence of grace). So thoroughly does estrangement overturn the fundamental structure of things that the same negation that makes theism incredible also gives to the most essential quality of God, his love, the paradoxicality and incredibility of grace.

IV

Let us close this brief discussion of the dialectic of rationality, incredibility, and credibility by making further explicit why we speak of credibility and what we might mean by it. It should be clear by now that there are two major reasons for the distinction we have drawn between rationality and credibility. The first is the more formal reason that, as we have noted, a large part of the content of Christian belief concerns matters not derivable directly from the ontological structure of our finitude and so not entailed by even the most careful and systematic rational or empirical scrutiny of that structure. Estrangement, if the Christian view of it be correct, is a warping—through freedom—of that structure, not a necessary consequence of it; it cannot, therefore, be proved by means of a systematic delineation of that structure—for "proof" involves uncovering

the necessary connections of an assumed aspect of an ontological structure with other aspects. It is for this reason that
metaphysical descriptions of existence always appear abstract
in relation to the concreteness of existence: either they outline its essential structure and miss its actual estrangement;
or they depict its estrangement, take that for the essential
structure, and so miss the creative elements within it. In any
case, if rationality connotes what can be philosophically
demonstrated—and that has been our use of the term—then
only the theistic component is "rational" in that sense, and
the symbolic descriptions of estrangement and of its resolution in grace remain beyond the scope of rationality so defined.

The second reason is closely associated with the first but
is more existential. As we have noted, concrete existence is
a mixture of creative, essential elements: destiny, freedom,
and possibility (and within them the work of providence), on
the one hand, with aspects of estrangement, fatedness, self-
destruction, and meaninglessness, on the other. Since in
historical being this mixture arises not out of necessity but
out of the compound of destiny and freedom, its character,
the balance of the two contrasting components, is at each
moment undecided, as is its ultimate issue. Thus is history
a diachronic drama and not a synchronic logical or entailed
system, a drama whose ultimate intelligibility and meaning
is at each moment both partly manifest and partly obscured.
Unintelligibility as well as intelligibility, mystery as well
as meaning are ingredient in the concreteness of personal
and historical being. No clear vision of either the structure,
the pattern, or the outcome of this drama is thus possible
from within its midst. If such an overall pattern is presumed,
it will be, as noted, at best an abstraction from this duality,
a premature closing of the contest, and at worst an assignation
of meaning from one partial viewpoint and thus ideological.
All total visions, therefore, and Christianity is one of them,
are held as much by faith as by persuasive insight—though
both grounds are there. And all of them, if they are to be self-
critical of their own ideological temptations and pretensions,
must recognize essentially this inability to grasp the whole

with demonstrable certainty and objective clarity. Though
ontology has a vital role in the understanding of history, any
comprehension of history as a whole, and so any *theological*
understanding, has the form of a global myth and not of a
systematic ontology; and such total views are, as Calvin said,
more matters of confidence than of certainty. If Christian
belief as a total view does not recognize its own status as credible
rather than demonstrable ("scientific" as the Marxists say of
theirs), it will, as has often happened, appear more as an
abstract idealism or as a pretentious idolatry than as a healing
grasp of a mystery beyond any clear and definitive comprehension.

The existential meaninglessness resulting from estrangement penetrates deeply, moreover, into the formal possibility
of theism as rational. For, as we have noted, in the case of each
phase of temporal being, the formal possibility of theism
depends upon a metaphysical inference—namely that *if* it is
to be intelligibly understood, finitude must be understood
as created, upheld, and guided by a divine ground. But the
possibility, legitimacy, and meaningfulness of such an inference can itself be questioned, as much contemporary philosophy has done. The reason for this questionableness is
that such inferences beyond the given—i.e., beyond the immediate reality of destiny, of freedom, and of possibility—
presuppose that being is throughout characterized by rationality, that being is logos as well as power, else logic and the
language of inference have no relevance beyond empirical
verification. If this be so, then a deep cultural or personal
experience of estrangement and so of the irrationality and
meaninglessness of historical being can in turn obscure this
intuition of the logos of being and render the foundations
of theistic rationality, i.e., the possibility of metaphysical
inference, ungrounded and so problematic. An intuition of
fundamental order, itself no more than credible, grounds and
establishes the possibility of metaphysical inference and so
of theistic rationality. Its preservation in the midst of estrangement can depend—though in bouyant ages it need not—on
the credibility of religious faith as a whole, which is why in

our day natural theology tends to prosper in seminaries, religious groups, and among their representatives, however "purely rational" or "purely philosophical" it may seek to present itself.

To say that the total system of Christian symbols is not rational in the sense of philosophically demonstrable is not, however, to maintain that it is irrational. For it is, as we have argued, credible: It can satisfy the mind as a valid symbolic thematization and description of the totality of concrete experience as no other global viewpoint can. As many contemporaries have urged, the criteria of its credibility are coherence among its major symbolic elements and adequacy to the contours of concrete experience taken as a whole. One can also add the theological requirement to be "appropriate," that is, faithful to the symbolic tradition within scripture and the historical interpretation of the Christian community.

The tricky word in this formula is, of course, 'adequacy'. How does one show that a particular point of view is adequate to the general contours of experience if it be granted that that viewpoint cannot be "proved" from experience? Obviously the answer is that the symbols which are said to be adequate must be shown to "fit" the shape of the experience they claim adequately to thematize. But the difficulty is that what that shape is taken to be—what are to me "the facts"—is itself in significant part determined by the symbolic structure with which experience is interpreted, and there is no uninterpreted experience. Thus is there what has been called the "theological circle" in relation to all foundational symbolic systems; and thus are arguments about adequacy—when one is considering interpretations of personal, historical, or social being as a whole—inevitably circular and inconclusive, each debate bringing forth not only a different symbolic complex but also a different constellation of common facts to prove the adequacy of that complex. Despite these difficulties, however, I believe it can be shown that a Christian interpretation provides a clearer, more illuminative, and more complete access to the full character of personal and historical experience than any other viewpoint. Its symbols

together make intelligible our existence by depicting its
contours accurately, by omitting or glossing over none of
the negative or counter-factual aspects of that existence, and
by providing credible grounds for those forms of human
existence and of action that fulfill human potentialities rather
than shrink them. It leads to illumination, courage, and
creative praxis, and thus it is credible. Where proof is not
possible, it is, as Kierkegaard said, nevertheless important
for reason to show *why* demonstration is here not possible;
and we have added, it is important to establish the fullest
level of rationality, namely that of coherence and adequacy,
as an intellectual warrant for the viewpoint that is to be
believed. This theology can and must do—for nothing is
believed that is also not thought by the mind to be true, that
is not held to be credible.

One further word on the conditions and character of credibility. Since, as we have argued, the rationality of Christian
belief is itself dialectically intertwined with its incredibility
and its credibility, it seems to me to follow that both that
rational component and the credible component are themselves dependent—if either one is to be credible—on what
we might call *intimations* in experience of the full scope of
Christian faith. It has been argued—by myself and others—
that the rationality of the theistic claim appears as rational
only to those who are aware of, or open to, a dimension of
ultimacy and sacrality in their existence which that rational
component seeks to explicate conceptually. And we have here
made the further point that the rationality of metaphysical
inference is itself grounded in a deep intuition of being as logos.
Now if we take our thesis of interdependence seriously—and
the point that theism may well be irrational and certainly
incredible to one caught in and overwhelmed by estrangement—
it follows that Christian theism is "rational" only to those who
also have intuitions of the estrangement of life on the one hand
and of its possibilities of healing despite that estrangement on
the other, i.e., to those who have intimations of both sin and
grace, though they surely do not need explicitly either to know
or to affirm those symbols. Experience and the intellectual

interpretation of experience are correlative categories and go together if they go at all. If, then, it is the total credibility of the Christian viewpoint that helps to give rationality to its rational component, then those experiences of estrangement and of rescue, of new possibilities in a seemingly fated situation—however unthematized into Christian symbols these intimations may be—are essential conditions for the whole dialectic if it is to reach its term in belief.

In conclusion, I would urge that Kierkegaard's caveat not be forgotten in discussing rationality and belief. We have concentrated on Christianity as a system of concepts: rational, incredible, and credible, as an intellectual "possibility" for our existence. We have not considered the deeper existential questions of the conditions for its reduplication into our existence, as a thought-form qualifying our life—nor how that relation in turn qualifies its credibility for us. It seems to me that these difficult questions—bracketed so far—cannot be totally set aside. If theism be considered valid, a participating sense of the working of the divine in our existence is an element in that sense of validity; if estrangement be taken seriously as a symbol, then a consciousness of sin in ourselves and our own is its necessary condition; if the gospel of redemption be considered credible, then experience of its reality, commitment to its demands and promises, and enactment of its implications in praxis are each intimately and immediately involved. Christianity is also, to be sure, a series of ideas set into symbolic terms, and it can be considered, criticized, defended, and re-shaped in that light. But the relevance, meaning, and validity of those symbols appear only if those symbols communicate through themselves the presence of the divine and if they are reduplicated in enactment and in existence and not just in aesthetic possibility. For these reasons the term 'credible' takes on deeper dimensions than merely rational coherence and experiential adequacy. It becomes the important intellectual side, the side of the mind, of faith, and of love as the deepest qualifications of our existence as a whole—which is after all what both rationality and belief are all about.

Religious Belief and Rationality

DAVID B. BURRELL, C.S.C.

"Talk about rationality can get very confusing—unless the things with which [reason] deals are also included."—Robert Pirsig, Zen and the Art of Motorcycle Maintenance, *p. 90.*

If religious belief is in fact belief in God, and if God is taken to be "the beginning and end of all things, and of reasoning creatures especially," then such belief must constitute an orientation of one's entire life.[1] Furthermore, if we allow ourselves to be guided by this nominal definition of God, we must acknowledge that the source and goal of all things cannot be one of those things, so God cannot be among the objects we talk about. Adjudicating the truth of statements about divinity will be strange business indeed. Talk about the rationality of believing in God becomes even more confusing when we begin trying to delineate what one is believing in.

Given such elusive parameters, one can see why questions regarding the rationality of religious belief easily shade into asking whether believing in God is a reasonable thing to do. That is, a line of questioning which looks first to the truth of certain claims begins imperceptibly to ask about the prudence of holding them to be true. The straightforward way to ascertain whether it is rational to believe p would be, of course, to determine whether or not p were true. If someone could show p to be the case, then it would be rational for that same person to believe p. One might also want to argue that it would be rational for someone else to believe p as well, secure in the knowledge that more astute inquirers had successfully shown p to be the case.

But these banalities are beside the point when it comes to belief in God, where the object in question *ex professo* out-reaches our demonstrative equipment. Belief in God certainly presupposes believing that God exists, but also entails so much more that an independent proof of God's existence would not be able to function as a foundation for believing in God. This observation amounts to a grammatical fact, following as it does from the intentionality appropriate to believing in God. The God one worships—like the creator who sees that everything is good—cannot be so embraced as to find itself presupposed in an explanatory scheme. We cannot insist that it *must* be there, as we do with theoretic entities, nor of course will we be able to pick it out. How could the creator of *all* things leave a distinguishing mark like Friday's footprints? Or if that were possible, how would we recognize the mark to be divine?

The upshot of these logical observations leaves us with faith as the sole appropriate epistemic attitude for relating to divinity. That is, we identify God to lie at the limit of our powers of conceiving things, so that we can at best *believe* in God. On this account, the classical enterprise of proving God's existence cannot be seen as a way of offering independent access to divinity, but must be understood as a way of justifying religious belief. Calling attention to certain epistemic facts can allow us to judge it reasonable to believe in a God we cannot understand. By testing the limits of our understanding in a disciplined and reflexive way, we can see that it would not be unreasonable to believe all this to be grounded in a single divine principle. Believing would be a prudent activity, not for the gains it promises, but because it fulfills a certain penchant for understanding.

Using Aquinas' treatment as a classical instance, I shall show that construing the proofs in this manner does not amount to a novel interpretation so much as a return to their original intent. Aquinas proposes them to test for (*probare*) God's existence, not to *demonstrate* it.[2] That is, he wants to lead us to reflect on the conditions required for us to *use* various explanatory schemes. His point is that the actual use of one or another framework for understanding or assessing the world presupposes an originative source. In contemporary language, each of the "proofs" exhibits an instance of "pragmatic implication"—not the sort of stuff of which ordinary demonstrations are made.[3]

Yet such a mode would be appropriate in attempting to deal rationally with divinity, for it amounts to showing how one who uses a working explanatory framework is thereby committed to something beyond that framework—something which functions in respect to the world so explained as divinity is said to function with respect to the world *tout court*: its originative source. On this way of construing the activity of testing for God's existence, we would not succeed in demonstrating that there is a God, nor would we have sought to do so. We would rather be probing the ways we employ to understand the world to see whether our use of them presupposes something beyond their capacity to formulate: a unitary source.

Since this mode of argumentation is so elusive, it is difficult to say when it is successful. For one thing, we are too little experienced with the maneuver itself of laying bare "pragmatic implications" to be very well versed in assessing individual arguments. Furthermore, to try to ascertain what may be presupposed in using a comprehensive explanatory framework pushes one's reflective capacities to the limit. So it may be very difficult to determine whether such a maneuver is ever successful—even after one is clear that we are not setting out to demonstrate God's existence.

On the other hand, it is possible to argue that the effort to test our explanatory schemes in this fashion can contribute indirectly to justifying belief in God. The very attempt to construct arguments so reflexive as these develops intellectual skills seldom called upon. Moreover, these skills engender an acquaintaince with the exercise of understanding itself, for the presuppositions alluded to are at once epistemic and existential. They amount to the conditions for understanding which Augustine experienced, in an idiom derived from the

Platonists with whom he had come in contact. That idiom, together with the experience it helped to articulate, offered him a language for divinity which cleared the way for his subsequent belief in God.[4]

The burden of my thesis will be that the so-called "proofs" for God's existence play a role predisposing one to religious belief. It is a useful role, and to understand it well allows one to address the issue of the rationality of such belief with some clarity. But these proofs are not intended as demonstrations, nor do they function as foundational to belief in God. They may be said, however, to offer a kind of justification for such belief. But since the notions of *foundation* and of *justification* themselves remain quite unclear, I shall have to offer a plausible account of each in defending the basic thesis regarding the "proofs."

1. Classical Views

I shall consider four traditional approaches to the issue of God's existence. Two of them directly address the question—those of Anselm and Aquinas—two approach it more by indirection—those of Augustine in the *Confessions* and Kant in the "Transcendental Dialectic." Of Anselm and Aquinas I will be asking: What was each of them up to in coming forward with proofs for God's existence? In an effort to answer that question, I will be asking whether it helps to relate their efforts to the task of justifying religious belief. Finally, as a way of locating the effort more precisely, I will inquire what it would be like to be successful in "proving" God's existence—and whether a successful "proof" would also offer justification for believing in such a God? Augustine and Kant will prove more helpful in answering these latter questions, and so in locating the enterprise.

1.1 Augustine

In his *Confessions*, Augustine does not expressly take up the task of proving God's existence so much as he monitors the different ways in which the question of God poses itself to an inquirer at different times in his life. The inquirer is himself, of course, and the shape of the God-question shifted as his set of concerns came to configure themselves differently. In Augustine's own intellectual odyssey, the problems he found in conceiving divinity ran parallel to those which beset him in trying to explain the origin of evil. This particular juxtaposition of issues is familiar enough in the tradition of Hebrew and Christian thought, yet another individual need not link them as Augustine did. His more fundamental point, however, regarding the way the question of God changes its shape with the overall configuration of our concerns, is especially germane to an inquiry into the rationality of religious belief.

What Augustine's narrative suggests is that "rationality" is too remote a notion to offer an actual context for inquiry. If speaking of *rationality* is to speak of norms for discourse, we would soon have to discriminate among these. A recognizable set of norms might be called "formal," and these would comprise rules for argument generally. Yet another set, however, which might be called "material," would formulate an entire set of decisions-cum-practices which go to make up a coherent way of life. To speak of a practice as *rational* certainly includes material as well as formal norms, yet the expression "rationality" usually pretends to a set of norms which would pervade every way of life.

The transcendentals, for example—good, true, and beautiful —name concerns which characterize and even shape any particular way of life, but these concerns will not all be realized by the same set of procedures. Indeed, analogous expressions like these offer a way of understanding how different ways of life are possible, for they allow us to comprehend them as ways of life and yet understand how differently they might be arranged. So Augustine moved from one set of concerns to another pursuing the same question, and yet retrospectively would show us how the shape of the question was altered.

Since the God-question is a limiting question, any attempt to show its relevance to a particular way of life will have to address the very shape of that way of life. Yet as a question which addresses the heart as well as the mind—"and God saw

which addresses the heart as well as the mind—"and God saw that
it was good"—it will concern more than merely formal rules for
discourse. So any attempt to show that God exists by indicating
how the reality of God would make a difference to one's way of
life, would have to address the concerns shaping that way of life.
By calling our attention to this fact, Augustine's *Confessions*
opens up many possible strategies and also suggests that we look
back on the classical "proofs" as exemplifying some of them.

1.2 Anselm

Anselm's preoccupation with finding "one single argument
that for its proof [*ad se probandum*] required no other save
itself, and that by itself would suffice to prove [*ad astruendum*]
that God really exists," reflects the fascination of his age for the
power of logic. That argument would have to respond to the
shape of the object intended, which he goes on to articulate:
"that He is the supreme good needing no other and is He whom
all things have need of for their being and well being, and also to
prove [*ad astruendum*] whatever we believe about the Divine
Being."[5] The aim of the argument will be to show that whoever
thinks of such a divine being must thereby affirm these things
to be true of it. All such a form of argument needed was an
appropriate formula.

This formula, Anselm recounts, "began to force itself upon
me more and more pressingly" just as "I was about to give up
what I was looking for as something impossible to find." He
needed a formula which captured enough of what his people
believed God to be to serve as a "nominal definition," and yet
was sufficiently cogent to yield a *reductio* proof of the features
noted: existence, supreme good needing no other, creator and
provider—and whatever else we believe of God. Put so suc-
cinctly, the project reveals the characteristic medieval strategy
for ferreting out the "real" definition from among any number
of ("nominal") contenders: That formula from which one can
deduce the features recognized to be *proper* to the item in
question will afford us *real* understanding of that item.[6]

Anselm's own description of his task certainly relativizes
the existence-feature, as does the composition of the work
itself: Three chapters are devoted to showing that this God

must exist, and twenty-two to elaborating the rest of "what we believe about the Divine Being." Gaunilo, of course, zeroes in on the existence-proof, so Anselm is constrained to elaborate that section in reply to his objections. Furthermore, there *is* something basic about *existence*, if only in that everything else we say about an object normally presumes that it exists; and unless the context is explicitly fictional, the failure of this presumption renders everything else pointless. These observations are beyond dispute, and the order of Anselm's treatment suggests that they guided his work as well. What remains questionable, however, is whether Anselm's primary goal was to prove that God existed, and further, whether *that* proof would be considered foundational to religious belief.

Given the curious logical primacy of existence, and the volume of subsequent debate over the propriety of a *reductio* proof of the matter, it is natural for us to presume that Anselm set out above all to prove that God exists. But the fact that he paid little or no attention to the logical peculiarties of '——— exists', allowing the range of 'greater' (in 'that-than-which-nothing-greater-can-be-thought') to extend over this feature along with all other relevant ones, suggests that we should attend more closely to his own description: "one single argument that . . . by itself would suffice to prove . . . whatever we believe about the Divine Being." The accent here would not be on 'believe' but on 'whatever', with the stated features—existence, supreme good, creator and provider—offered by way of illustration.

If we were to read Anselm in this way, we would find ourselves placing his enterprise squarely within the Augustinian project which he expressly owns: "the point of view of one trying to raise his mind to contemplate God and seeking to understand what he believes" (Preface). Furthermore, we would do so without giving one inch to an anachronistic charge (or defense) of fideism.[7] In fact, such a reading would have to conclude that Anselm's specific project was to offer what he (and his times) construed to be a rational foundation for religious belief. This would require that the object believed could be made intelligible, which one would do by constructing a formula from which any thinking person would be able to deduce the proper features of the object in question.

To do so would be to have met the formal requirements for scientific knowledge delineated in Aristotle's *Posterior Analytics.*[8] That is, the God of Christian faith-cum-theological-reflection would have been shown to be intelligible, and believing in that God vindicated as a rational endeavor. Whether or not this God is the true God was not at issue; in fact, even the features considered to be proper were so named from the history of Christian theological reflection. All that was at issue was the intelligibility of the object and hence the justifiability of believing as Christians do. That such a God *must* exist represents part of its intelligibility, and there is internal evidence that Anselm was interested more in the formal fact that God *must* exist than in the sheer fact of his existence.[9] Indeed, the single result of Anselm's proof (or proofs) which has been able to withstand the scrutiny of centuries is stated by way of concluding the three chapters devoted to using the formula to show that God "really exists":

> Whoever really understands this [formula] understands clearly that this same being so exists that not even in thought can it not exist. Thus whoever understands that God exists *in such a way* cannot think of Him as not existing. (chap. IV, italics mine)

To italicize the words I have, makes this final statement a clear tautology. But it takes a great deal of speculation about Anselm's epistemological "realism" to pretend that he is not uttering a closing tautology. So it seems simpler to let the statement stand that way and to summarize the achievement of Anselm's initial chapters in his own words: "And certainly this being so truly exists (*sic vere est*) that it cannot even be thought not to exist (*esse*)" (chap. III). Anselm's formula allowed him to deduce a formal feature of divinity which would characterize it uniquely: "everything else there is, except You alone, can be thought of as not existing" (chap. III). Aquinas will adopt this feature as formally defining divinity and hence anything which might be said about God: to be God is to be. He will not presume the connections Anselm did between this

definitional use of 'to be' and the curious predicate '———
exists'. But then Aquinas had available to him the sophisticated
legacy of logical analysis and speculative grammar which
predecessors like Anselm had helped to refine.

On this reading, Anselm set out to offer a kind of justification
for religious belief, in the form of a "single argument . . . that by
itself would suffice to prove [*ad astruendum*] . . . whatever we
believe about the Divine Being" (Preface). The argument
purported to show "that God really exists," along with other
classical properties of the Christian God. The role of such an
argument was to show that one could think coherently about
the God whom one worshipped as Lord of heaven and earth. In
that precise sense, Anselm offered a proof for God's existence
intended as well to justify the beliefs of Christian faithful.

1.3 Aquinas

With the benefit of these dialectical exercises of Anselm,
as well as a century of concern for speculative grammar, Aquinas
could take over the central achievement of the *Proslogion* as
the keystone for this treatment of divinity. The feature which
at once defines divinity and assures uniqueness is a syntactical
feature: in God essence and *esse* must be identified.[10] Furthermore, this formal feature lays down a grammatical condition
which any statement about God must observe. So Aquinas will
take pains to show that the other formal features characterizing
discourse about divinity are equivalent to this one: that God is
good, limitless, unchangeable, and one, become so many ways
of saying that to be God is to be.[11] Whatever revelation may lead
us to say about God must conform to this fundamental syntactical condition which Aquinas calls "simpleness."

We have seen how Aquinas' formula translates with characteristic economy the upshot of Anselm's efforts: "that this
same being so exists that not even in thought can it not exist,"
for its very nature is to be. Yet the intervening two centuries
contributed a good deal of semantic sophistication, so that
Aquinas was not tempted by surface grammar to identify this
'to be' with the fact that God exists. The curious fact that

existence was identical with the divine essence could show the uniqueness of divinity, but should not obscure the fact that asking what something is, and whether it is, ask two distinct questions. So a separate inquiry must be launched to determine whether God exists.

Aquinas makes this point explicitly in a way which has only succeeded in confusing the issue: "the proposition *Deus est* is self-evident in itself, for . . . its subject and predicate are identical, since God is his own existence" (1.2.1). Closer attention to syntactical rules of composition would have reminded him that the 'to be' of 'God is to be' and the 'is' of 'God is' play very different roles. And it is this fact which makes him go on to insist: "because what it is to be God is not evident to us, the proposition is not self-evident to us, and needs to be made evident." In other words, we have no way of knowing how to use 'to be' as a predicate noun, yet we can try to see how one might be led to say that there *is* a God.

Aquinas' strategy here is guided by the sophisticated criterion of simpleness, for one must know what it is he is setting out to find. The given to us inquirers, however, is a nominal definition: "the beginning and end of all things and of reasoning creatures especially" (1.2 Intro.). The only thing we know, then, is that everything derives from this source, and it cannot itself be among those derived things. What paths of inquiry could possibly lead to something from which everything else originates? If we are to take the five ways Aquinas offers as *bona fide* examples, we must bring to light conditions presupposed by accepted forms of investigation into the world about us. Some of these forms will be at work in any investigation, and Aquinas wants to show how we cannot use any of them without presupposing a first principle proper to each form—and this first principle would offer an inadequate yet plausible rendition of "the beginning and end of all things."

The forms of investigation Aquinas considers are change, causation, necessity/contingency, normative assessment, and finality in nature. His arguments purport to show that each of these *in its actual use* presupposes a first, "and this is what everybody understands by God" (1.2.3). Yet these arguments have proven to be quite fragile. Aquinas' strategy has proven to be unconvincing, in that we all seem able to forge and to use accounts of change and causation without reference to a first principle. Similarly, we can make sense out of the logical notions of necessity and contingency, as well as make assessments and account for orderedness in nature, without demanding "something which must be," or a source of goodness, or an author of nature directing it to its goal.

Furthermore, if we were to be convinced that none of these forms of inquiry could be employed without presupposing a *first* in each, that first would have to belong to the series so defined—as the "first cause of the change," to adopt the first way. And such a one could hardly qualify as "the beginning and end of all things," since the mode of argument leading us to it placed it among the changing things themselves. This should be clear with reference to the other ways as well: causation, necessity/contingency, normative assessment, and finality in nature. If we can discern the purposes of God in natural process, then we must claim to know more than Aquinas' tradition would allow; yet if it is simply orderedness that forces itself upon us, why must that yield divinity? And so on for the others.[12]

The most we can say at this point for Aquinas, then, is that he made the best of Anselm's discovery regarding God's manner of being by turning it into the formally defining feature of divinity. He also understood that such a use of 'to be' could not do double duty as a proof that there indeed is a God. So far as his strategy for answering the question "whether there is a God," we can at least conclude that he did not execute it satisfactorily. Whether the strategy itself remains a fruitful one shall have to wait further consideration.

1.4 Kant

Kant is celebrated, of course, for having successfully challenged the goals and strategies of classical metaphysics. Of these, the endeavor to prove God's existence must be considered central. If it appears to have been quite secondary to the medieval agenda, it had become one of the defining goals of a branch of metaphysics—theodicy—by Kant's time. His sustained effort to show how this enterprise led into hopeless antinomies could be considered part of his larger plan to secure room for faith while establishing the mutual credibility of philosophy and of science. By removing discourse about divinity to the domain of practical reason, he meant to locate religious faith where it could properly develop, as well as save it from the vagaries of groundless metaphysical speculation.

The purposes of this inquiry demand that we bracket Kant's constructive attempts to show how God is presupposed in the exercise of practical reason. Examining these would require that we acknowledge his way of distinguishing "practical" from "pure" reason, and that maneuver would divert our energies from attempting to shed fresh light on the classical enterprise. I shall rather content myself with calling attention to a series of leading assertions which Kant makes in the Appendix to the "Transcendental Dialectic" section of his first *Critique of Pure Reason*.[13]

In this section Kant deals with notions like those which the tradition since Aristotle had identified as "transcendentals": one, true, and good. Kant focuses on *unity*. He has two things to say about it: it is not a constitutive principle of understanding but a merely regulative one. By itself, that is, *unity* cannot bring forth an object, even if any object with which we concern ourselves must be able to be *singled out* for investigation. Understanding presupposes unity: "we must endeavor, wherever possible, to bring in this way systematic unity into our knowledge" (A 650, B 678). Yet this unity, as it is, remains the transcendental condition of something's being an object; and "one cannot say, for example, 'There are objects', as one might say, 'There are books'" (as Wittgenstein remarks in *Tractatus* 4.1272).

So Kant is quite ready to admit that "the law of reason which requires us to seek for this unity is a necessary law, since without it we should have no reason at all, and without reason no coherent employment of the understanding, and in the absence of this no sufficient criterion of empirical truth" (A 651, B 679). Hence Kant's entire conception of knowledge leaves him with "no option save to presuppose the systematic unity of nature as objectively valid and necessary." He is quick to point out, of course, that it is illusory to pretend that this presupposition, necessary as it is, yields a determinate object. We will speak of the self, the cosmos, and God, yet "they ought not to be assumed as existing in themselves, but only as having the reality of a schema—the schema of the regulative principle of the systematic unity of all knowledge of nature" (A 674, B 702). 'Self', 'world', and 'God' are but names we give to the fact that our scientific inquiry must presuppose an inquiring subject, a determinate object, and a ground for both.

In response to the question, however, "can we, on such grounds, assume a wise and omnipotent Author of the world?" Kant insists: "*Undoubtedly* we may; and we not only may, but *must*, do so. But do we then extend our knowledge beyond the field of possible experience? *By no means*. All that we have done is merely to presuppose a something, a merely transcendental object, of which, as it is in itself, we have no concept whatsoever" (A 697, B 725). In fact, Kant notes, if we do try such an argument to come up with a deity, we have the god of deism: "the idea of something which is the ground of the highest and necessary unity of all empirical reality" (A 675, B 703). Yet "what has justified us in adopting the idea of a supreme intelligence as a schema of the regulative principle is precisely this greatest possible systematic and purposive unity—a unity which our reason has required as a regulative principle that must underlie all investigation of nature" (A 699, B 727).

So an inquirer must presuppose unity but cannot thereby presume that he has come up with an object which can otherwise be named. For we do not identify objects from their unity but from the kinds of things they are. Yet the demand for unity is *really*—and not *merely*—regulative. If Kant is to be consistent, what is presupposed to the understanding of an object, whether "regulatively" or "constitutively," contributes to that object's being the object it is. He rightly contrasts *constitutive* with *regulative* principles to denote levels of constituent factors, but his tendency to call one *objective* and the other *subjective*

(A 680, B 708) undermines his observation that "we have no option save to presuppose the systematic unity of nature as objectively valid and necessary" (A 651, B 679). We cannot pretend to use this notion of *unity* to come up with an object, yet the demand for unity is no less real for that.

Kant's struggle with transcendentals like *unity* might help us understand what is going on in the endeavor to test or probe for signs of divinity. We cannot look to find God in the world, so maybe God is the presupposition of the world—or of discoursing about a world. If so, God will not be an object of an indentifiable sort but will be as real as the exercise of inquiring into nature and the understanding of objects which it yields. Kant has elucidated the movement in its starkest form, but is not this move common to all of Aquinas' five ways? Could we not regard the stipulation that "we must stop somewhere" as a simple way of expressing this transcendental demand for "systematic unity"? That is, the very use of the explanatory schemes associated with change or causality presupposes that we be able to think the process coherently. A simple way of proposing that is to think of a series and stipulate a first. We have already remarked, of course, that the God Aquinas is looking for could never be the first in a series. Now we can add that there are other ways of assuring that one's notion of causation is coherent.

Yet this comparison of Aquinas' strategy with Kant's observations about the necessity of regulative principles for inquiry may enlighten us regarding the endeavor of testing for God's existence. What if the recurrent form such tests took were to attempt to lay bare the presuppositions of a comprehensive human practice? Aquinas chose forms of explanation and of assessment; Kant elevated the consideration to understanding itself. Kant's move helped us to see what was going on in Aquinas' ways but also distracted us by its attempt at utter generality. What if we were to turn to any practice which claimed to relate a person to the world in a critical and corrigible manner? The form which an argument for God's existence would take would be to show how such a practice presupposed belief in a divinity. Or better, it would try to show that among alternative practices, those which could be shown to presuppose belief in God proved to relate us to reality more adequately.

2. Foundations for and Justification of Religious Belief

By surveying these classical ways of leading one to affirm God's existence, I have been working to correct a pervasive misunderstanding of the intent of the classical ways. None of them attempts to prove that God exists, as if to turn up something which we had not previously noted. They do not conceive reason's role to be one of establishing the fact of an object on which every other fact might rest. Even if we regard these ways as exercises in a "foundational" use of reason, they are not foundational in so crude a sense as that.

In fact, what the "proofs" try to do is the reverse of their caricature. They are rather concerned to show that the coherent exercise of reason—to understand whatever presents itself to be understood—itself presupposes a [belief in a] first principle, which is what Jews and Christians affirm to be God. The explanatory functions of reason need not be *based* on a divinity, as though each explanation could be traced back to the fact of God as an initial premise. Explanatory schemes have a logic of their own which need not postulate God as thesis or hypothesis. This fundamental feature of explanatory systems finds expression in Kant's distinguishing *constitutive* from *regulative* principles, and in Aquinas' assertion that "whatever is moved is moved by another." So we do not need to establish that God exists before we can explain why things happen as they do.

It is rather that our use of reason to explain takes its impetus from a unity more comprehensive than any scheme can account for, much as particular discussions of justice invariably reflect a cosmic sense of justice which defies formulation.[14] Since that more comprehensive unity cannot be forced into an explanatory scheme, one can only believe it to be the case. Yet our continued use of particular explanatory frameworks would be pointless without such a belief. If this be the structure of the classical ways which set out to "prove" God's existence, they do not pretend to deliver divinity as the first in an explanatory chain. Rather, we begin with the very practice of explaining, only to find that such a practice presupposes belief in a first principle quite beyond its ken: either to explain or to contain as a constituent of any explanation.

It is not the consistency of an explanation which is at stake, but rather our coherent use of the explanatory schemes we have and have shown to be consistent. In Kant's terms, the concepts of the understanding which constitute scientific objects presuppose for their application the regulative principles of reason. Yet we only realize this fact in retrospect, as it were, as we reflect on the ways we use explanatory concepts. Aquinas put the point quite crudely when he relied on the image of a chain of movers to insist that there must be a first, lest no movement eventuate. He uses another image—that of a stick moved by a hand—to convey instrumentality, and some have exploited the second image to read him as demanding a first principle to establish the fact (or category) of motion itself. On my interpretation, however, both images can be taken *as images*, to convey what we find on reflection to be presupposed to one's use of schemes purporting to explain the motion of bodies.

2.1 Foundations for Religious Belief

What is at stake here is a way of understanding *foundation* which may help us thread a way through various polemics. It is commonplace to expect that proofs of God's existence be presented as a foundation for religious belief. The expectation is natural enough, since prayer to or discourse about God must presuppose that God exists. Were there nothing to address, praying would be pointless and illusory. Yet the notion of *foundation*, like the expression '—— is based on ——', is notoriously ambiguous, so ambiguous, indeed, that one can easily be tempted to eschew any quest for foundations and to seek intellectual legitimation elsewhere.

The metaphor remains attractive, however, so long as we feel compelled to ask for the *grounds* on which an assertion is *based.* It is misleading, of course, in that a foundation must be laid down first, as the initial step in constructing a building. So one easily presumes that God must *first* be shown to exist before we can legitimately engage in those practices associated with belief in God. In fact, however, the situation is quite the reverse. It is those who participate in such practices who come to appreciate how intimately these practices are intertwined with a conviction of the reality of God. When they are not, these cease to be religious practices and become ritual maintenance-structures of the status quo. The Gospel polemic against scribes and pharisees dramatizes this point and confirms just how rooted are religious practices in the reality of God.

The phenomenology of these things does not contradict so much as it confirms the logic of the matter. Proofs for God's existence are not very helpful stepping stones to religious belief, even though religious practice requires God's reality for its authenticity. Similarly, a successful proof for God's existence is hardly required to legitimize scientific inquiry, even when the proof-strategy normally seeks to show how an affirmation of God is presupposed to explanatory uses of reason. For *presupposition* is a tricky affair, and "pragmatic presupposition" is trickier still. As P. F. Strawson showed in his treatment of *existence*, the (extensional) logical rubric of *necessary condition* is not adequate to capture the status of those things we actually presuppose in our speech and our behavior.[15] And since we ordinarily render *foundation* by *necessary condition*, the confusion is easily compounded.

It would be as plausible, for example, to note that explanatory practice undergirds the affirmation of a more comprehensive unity, as it would to regard that affirmation as grounding the practice. Similarly, one might well be struck by the coherence of a religious life before inquiring into its presuppositions, and even continue to be more persuaded by the life than the explanations it gives for itself. It was a commonplace among medievals, of course, to note how the path of discovery mirrored that of analysis, and that one needed always to bear in mind whether he was coming or going. Something of that is at work here; a heedless use of the *foundation* metaphor often overlooks that elementary admonition. Let us look more closely then, with this distinction in mind, at the role which proofs might play in offering some grounds for religious belief.

2.11 A Constructive Proposal

My proposal, at once interpretative and constructive, takes the following form:

(1) the activities ingredient to rational inquiry can be shown to presuppose an operative belief in some overarching unity;

(2) the practices of religious faith require a living connection with divine reality at work in us and in the world;

(3) while it is reasonable to begin from the practices mentioned (rational inquiry or religious faith) and to trace what each presupposes, one can try to identify as one reality what both presuppose, and so construct a path from the practice of rational inquiry, through its presupposition and that of religious belief, to the practices of faith. It is unlikely, certainly, that anyone would actually follow such a path to its goal, but its very presence lends some plausibility to thinking of the endeavor called "proving God's existence" as foundational to religious belief.

Schematically:

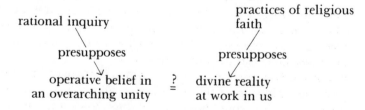

2.111 Transcendental Argument to Presuppositions

The two most controversial claims are clearly (1), that our practices of inquiry presuppose an effective belief in a unity

outreaching any single scheme, and that part of (3) which says
that one can plausibly identify that unity with the reality of
God. Let us examine them together, for both harbor many
potential confusions.

The first claim is designed to link the effectiveness of any
particular scientific inquiry to a pervasive belief in a unity
which no such inquiry could ever explain. That is the sense of
"presuppose" as it is used here, so that an effective belief becomes the engine of a successful inquiry. If such inquiries,
however, offer us paradigm instances of access to the world,
then the believed unity (which they presuppose) must in fact
obtain. This argument will remain suspect until we can better
clarify presupposition, but it certainly holds within the limits
of our uncertainty regarding the logico-pragmatic connection.
So one can move from an operative belief in unity to the unity
affirmed. A recent instance of such an argument is that offered
by Alastair McKinnon (in *Falsification and Belief*) for the
foundational assertion: "the world has an order."[16]

McKinnon notes that scientists seldom make such oracular
statements, but that one plausibly could do so in three distinct
contexts: (a) factual, (b) hortatory or self-instructive, and (c)
ontological-linguistic. The first arises "when he has just discovered a particular order," the second "when some strange
event has challenged his familiar conceptions," and the third
"when he is attempting to meet the philosophers' challenge
to defend the assumptions of his discipline" (p. 28).

The first is intended as a factual claim describing a particular
connection or law. While it relies on the analogous structure
latent in 'order' to mark the import of the discovery, this use of
'the world has an order' does not explicitly invoke the evaluative
reaches of that expression. But the other two uses do. McKinnon
describes the self-instructional use as a way in which a scientist
might steady himself in a situation which challenged his sure-
ties: "but things must fit together; after all, the world has an
order." This use would not admit of direct assessment as true
or false, for it intends to exhort, not to state. Yet the *order* referred to cannot be a particular order; it must be "order as such"
(p. 29). McKinnon dubs this use "heuristic"; I would simply

remind us that it is an explicitly analogous use.[17] It characterizes the third context as well, which transforms the exhortation into a claim.

The third use is most germane to our inquiry. McKinnon calls it *ontological-linguistic* to signal the fact that the assertion means to catch up an inquirer's reflective realization that his entire activity does in fact presuppose such a conviction. His characteristic intellectual practices would be pointless if the world lacked order. Yet none of them is adequate to articulate this order that each presupposes; and this is a grammatical point. That is, whatever the inquiry, it requires *as inquiry* certain configurational conditions if it is to be successful. Each inquiry attempts to spell out in particular what these are, yet every inquiry must presuppose *some* configuration to begin.

The order I am alluding to here reminds one of Kant's regulative unity. Its status remains curious, since the unity is indeterminate, yet indeterminacy cannot warrant calling such a presupposition "merely subjective," as Kant was wont to do. As a constituent, if not a constitutive, feature of inquiry, the unity presupposed cannot be different in status from particular inquiries and their objects. That is certainly the logic of transcendental argument, yet we never feel that such arguments quite warrant affirming the reality of these presuppositions. So we can appreciate Kant's ambivalence in the "Transcendental Dialectic." And the same doubts bedevil transcendental arguments to the reality of God: how can we identify the *order* presupposed by scientific inquiry with the divinity whose reality undergirds religious practice? And why should we?

Theologically speaking, we should not, of course, unless we are prepared to espouse a form of pantheism. A theologian would remind us at this point that the most we can be speaking of is the "order of creation"—what Genesis alluded to by insisting that "God saw that it was good" at the closing of each day's work. Moving from the other direction, as we have, it would be too quick to insist that order demands an orderer, however, even as it would be naive to presume that the "law of large numbers" has rendered such reasoning archaic. Order does require explanation whenever we find it, as random

selection only works within a determinate context. So the
assertion, however indeterminate, that the world has an order,
must leave a question. And the more we realize how our explanatory practice presupposes an order, the more determined
will we be in asserting there is one, and so the more pressing
will the question be: whence the order?

Philosophically speaking, we can go no further, it seems—
hence Kant's inconclusive ending of the *Critique of Pure
Reason*. We may regard this question as a leading one, certainly
and even locate it within a theological neighborhood; for the
indeterminate unity which evokes it can only be what theologians call the "order of creation."[18]Yet a presupposition
which evokes a question cannot establish the reality of divinity.
It can, however, legitimate discourse theological in character.
In that sense, the unity presupposed by the practice of explanatory inquiry can be said to offer a foundation for religious
discourse—even though the transcendental arguments which
bring such unity to light will not suffice to establish the
reality of God.

We can speak of such transcendental arguments offering a
foundation for religious discourse, however, in the measure
that they have introduced us into the logical domain proper to
theological assertions. These arguments cannot legitimize such
assertions, however, any more than knowing how to construct
a sentence in a language warrants our asserting it. So we are
left with a quite tenuous sense of *foundation*, and certainly
nowhere near what one was led to expect as a proof for God's
existence. If I am correct, however, in locating the generic
form of such proofs in the transcendental argument outlined,
they can claim nothing more than a grammatical beachhead
in theological territory. And that would already be a great deal
more than most philosophers would admit, given the un-
clarities surrounding arguments to and from presuppositions.

2.112 *Foundations: A Two-Way Metaphor*

Nevertheless, it remains appropriate to speak of a grammatical claim as foundational, so one can construct a path of sorts,

short of identifying this unity or order with divinity. **Again,** it is not a path anyone is likely to follow, precisely because one would have to cross the infinite gap from created order to creator, yet a path **is** discernable nonetheless. It may help to see through the path metaphor if we reflect on the ambiguities inherent in *foundations.* This metaphor has two clear and opposite primary senses: one pertinent to the contractor and the other to the archaeologist. The first lays a foundation before anything else, the second looks for one as a goal of his dig. The logic of a search for foundations is more archaeological, whereas we retain some expectations from them more akin to a contractor. It is these latter expectations which make us want to assure ourselves of God's existence *before* we can responsibly undertake religious practice. Yet we have seen that presuppositions need not function like initial premises, and often cannot, for they are insufficiently determinate to do so.

So the two directions characterizing the foundation-metaphor continue to work against each other, and easily foment a sharp polemic regarding the very enterprise. Hence one can regard the actual practice of scientific investigation as the foundation for the ontological-linguistic assertion that the world has an order—in the sense of the evidence or warrant adduced for such a statement. Alternatively, we can regard that assertion as foundational to explanatory inquiry, once we have shown how such inquiry presupposes a belief that the world has an order.

It is this latter, more archaeological sense of *foundation* which one is normally looking for, I suspect, coming as it does as the result of analysis. Yet while such a presupposition may be said to *ground* scientific inquiry, it does not warrant it in the sense of offering evidence in support of any specific inquiry; nor does it supply a premise which must be asserted before inquiring, as one of a set of premises from which the practice follows. In fact, the logical situation is a good deal less clear than that, so we cannot much expect that a more formal treatment will be able to clear up the ambivalence endemic to a quest for *foundations.*

If we can agree, however, that the attempt to locate presuppositions to practices answers most directly to the intent
of a quest for foundations, then we would be less tempted
to construct a single path from inquiry, through the order
it presupposes and a divine orderer, to religious practice.
We would rather be led to determine what religious practice
presupposes and see whether any analogies might be observed
between the God so worshipped and the unity tacitly sought.

2.12 God as Presupposed in Authentic Religious Practice

Just as one may argue that effective scientific inquiry presupposes an operative conviction that the world is ordered,
so genuine religious belief demands a lively faith in the
reality of God—and in that reality at work in us. The Gospels
do not argue for Jesus, but the Jesus they present *is* an argument for the reality of the God he calls "Father." Furthermore, the studied structure of each of the Gospels is intended
to bring the reader to acknowledge the authenticity of Jesus,
so that he can become the argument for God. We should not
expect to be able even to locate the divinity outside of religious
practice, much less provide a way of establishing God's
reality independent of those practices which are designed to
offer us access to God. If these practices and the communities
they form, however, present a way which is recognizably
liberating (in the manner which religion promises to be),
then we will be attracted to the God they worship and led to
inquire how such a divinity pervades the practices we have
come to cherish.

The intellectual movement described here is strictly parallel
to the form of argument used earlier, where a practice can
be seen to presuppose (pragmatically) a pervasive belief without which the practice would be pointless. Moreover, where
the practice can be seen to be effective, then the belief bears
the signs of a true belief. Scientific inquiry has been subjected
to a great deal more scrutiny than religious practice; and
science also enjoys paradigmatic status for giving us access
to reality, whereas religious practice has been relegated by

liberal thought to the intellectual limbo of privacy. That maneuver neatly avoids the question of truth or authenticity, leaving only the question whether one's belief is *satisfying*. So we are not in a favorable position from which to talk about criteria for authentic religious faith and practice. That cultural fact may help to explain why so many philosophers would think that an *independent* justification for religious belief should be sought, and even demanded, before one might responsibly believe.

2.2 *Justification of Religious Belief*

The notion and practice of *justification* turn out to be as elusive as the quest for foundations. Nor should that be surprising, since the two appear to be logical neighbors; the most acceptable justification for an assertion would certainly be one which laid bare its foundations. Yet *justifying* belief also promises, after a fashion, to enable us to believe—or so we often expect justifications to do. Recalling the two operative paradigms for *foundation*—constructed and archaeological—we tend spontaneously to think of justifications as required steps in a process of coming to believe, and so ask them to come first in a constructive activity.

These observations suggest a preliminary cut among justifications: *prospective* and *retrospective*. The first seeks to answer: Why should I undertake this activity? The second queries: What am I doing engaged in it? We want the activity of justifying to handle both types of question, yet we tend to accept the *prospective* form as paradigmatic. Similarly, in searching for foundations we knew we were on an archaeological dig, yet quickly wanted our findings to play a constructive role. So we want justifications to provide stepping stones to belief as much as to offer a plausible reason why. In a similar vein, one wants arguments for God's existence to have a certain persuasive force: to effect belief!

What if we were to recommend shifting the paradigm to retrospective justification? We would have to argue the point, of course, and the arguments would be cumulative.

They would remind us how abstract the prospective model is: that we are seldom in a situation of assuring our steps ahead of time. Usually we find ourselves already engaged, at least in part, and then look back to determine how the situation extends our own past coherently as well as opens us into a promising future. Where judgments of right/wrong, true/false are involved with the steps to be taken, we realize that we cannot judge adequately without tasting and that we need experiential reference points for drawing analogies. So it never quite makes sense to ask for assurance beforehand, yet we also need to know what it is we are getting into.

To explore the differences between paradigms, consider the following sets of questions and characteristic activities:

Prospective	*Retrospective*
probabilities of success: a legitimate risk?	what have I gained? learned? become?
cost benefit analysis	ongoing investment counsel
arguments in favor of entertaining a hypothesis	arguments confirming/ disconfirming a hypothesis

To lay out the differences is to notice similarities, of course, particularly between ongoing investment counsel and any analysis of benefits over costs. Indeed, that example leads one to suspect that if we were to assign a primacy, it would go to retrospective justification. We tend to assign antecedent probabilities on the basis of past successes or failures. Furthermore, focusing on prior justification tends to confuse *justifying* with "making certain." We have seen how easily the quest for foundations, begun as an analytic inquiry along archaeological lines, quickly becomes assimilated to a constructive process. Perhaps other less evident processes are at work in both cases, putting the quest for understanding at the service of a need for security. However that may be, it turns out to be more natural to accept the retrospective sense of justification as more basic than the prospective. While it may be tempting to academics to consider life as a series of decisions based on evidence, it makes more sense on reflection to see ourselves as attempting to understand the ways we find ourselves to be drawn.

Like anyone else, a believer finds himself situated in the midst of the fears and puzzles which beset a human life. If he is a reflective person who holds his religious faith along with other convictions, that faith, and his hold on it (or its hold on him), will continually be tested. It will be tested precisely in that area which faith shapes: our manner of relating to what is the case. If we remind ourselves that the way in which we relate to the world makes all the difference—"the world of a happy man is a different one from that of the unhappy man"—then we might begin to ask ourselves in what that difference consists.

Are we speaking merely about attitudes, i.e., postures we can assume or not at will? Or are we exploring the way in which the world includes the characteristic attitudes we assume towards it, paradoxical as that may sound? If the forces displayed in physical nature are indifferent to our fate, *we* are not—and cannot be. Yet in another sense of the term, we certainly qualify as part of nature. So nature (in this extended sense) is hardly indifferent to our fate; it is (i.e., we are) engaged in "negotiating" that very fate. And if we understand *convictions* to be those sets of beliefs which shape our (and our community's) response to the questions associated with our fate, then religious faith functions as just such a conviction set.[19]

In the retrospective sense of justification, we are continually justifying our set of beliefs by the manner in which they help us to relate to our own fate by rendering (1) a plausible account of the parameters of human existence—of birth, sex and death —which (2) offers the capacity to deal with these realities. Thus the central symbol of Jewish and Christian belief— that God created the universe—does not state a physical fact *about* the universe so much as it announces something like a "formal fact" about it. The belief that God created the universe cannot come up directly to be verified or falsified, yet the fact that one holds such a belief commits one to

adopting certain postures toward the world, notably that of
stewardship. At least the accounts of God's creating found
in the Hebrew scriptures do, and do so in such a way that a
posture of stewardship is germane to the account itself. That
is, the account of God's creating the universe is one which
includes intentional beings and their proper attitude towards
the universe as part of a created universe. When that attitude
is awry, the universe itself is said to be disordered.

Another way of putting this situation is to remind ourselves
that the world in which we live does not present itself as a bare
fact but comes complete with a "story." That "story" stands in
for the many practices which we learn throughout our life as
ways of relating to the world. These practices are often recom-
mended in actual stories, told us most effectively by persons
whose own characteristic set of attitudes displays their worth.
The world we accept is a storied world, and the degree of critical
acceptance we come to give it depends upon the capacity of the
accompanying story to enhance or to hinder the development
of both me and my world.[20]

One's understanding of one's self, one's individual and
shared destiny, is at stake in assessing the religious accounts
of the world, and those same accounts provide the parameters
which shape that self-understanding. There is no independent
standpoint from which one can justify a religious belief—once
we understand the role such a belief plays in shaping our basic
intentions toward the world. Yet there are different ways of
construing those basic intentions, and different versions of the
story, as well as different stories. The capacity to bring different
versions to bear on my life-project vicariously or imaginatively,
and so test my version, as well as to come to a more nuanced
understanding of my own version and the role it plays—all this
will be involved in the continual testing which I have called
"retrospective justification" of a religious belief.[21]

The criteria are not so much stated as displayed, much as
persons recommend themselves to us by the way they deal with
shared human predicaments, as a result of which·we want to
know what makes them what they are. Inquiries of this kind
turn up patterns—of a very analogous sort—which we hesitate

even to articulate, since the language must remain vague—e.g., "reconciliation of opposites." Furthermore, what recommends a characteristic way of acting is not the pattern it instantiates, but the way each individual performance offers us a richer understanding of the aforesaid "pattern." In other words, religious faith cannot recommend itself to us for its predictive power, but for its transforming power. For if it could succeed simply in predicting, it would fail to command the quality of engagement which it must demand—to be religious faith; although if it failed to offer some instances of actual transformation, it should have no claim on us whatsoever.[22]

But how can we adjudicate among engagements, or even more, among promises and accounts of transformation? The answer lies in the capacity of narrative to display how the religious patterns of understanding connect with those shared human concerns which are ingredient in "the good life." We learn how to distinguish melodrama from drama as well as to discriminate among dramatic forms and even to rank some as classics. So a narrative account lies open to scrutiny and offers us a way of determining whether a retrospective justification of religious belief is adequate or not. Indeed, classic narratives like Augustine's *Confessions* or Dante's *Divine Comedy* even offer paradigms for composing our own stories, for sifting relevant issues from irrelevant detail.

The fact that Augustine's autobiography relates a conversion, however, makes of it a clear justification for faith. What of alternative accounts—say the intensely autobiographical essays of Camus? Here again, the same criteria apply: Do these writings assist us in understanding and in negotiating those parameters of human life that we all share? Moreover, we may answer that question differently at different times in our own life, as Augustine's account avers. So the justification of religious belief will be an ongoing affair, as the characteristically religious questions arise for each of us in a new key as we encounter ourselves trying to make sense of the world we live in and our way of living in it. Once we see how narrative offers the mode appropriate to meeting these limiting questions, we will have become convinced that retrospective justification presents

a more realistic as well as a more demanding facet of the activity
of justifying belief.

3. A Successful "Proof"

Let us look back at the activity of proving God's existence
to see what profit we can draw from these considerations on
retrospective justification. What is it that the "proofs" can be
said to be doing if they cannot yield an object which in fact
exists? If we consider the form they hold in common, it is one
which tries to point out the inadequacy of current explanatory
schemes to meet the originating impulse to understand. So
I would class a contemporary critique of psychology—like
Becker's *Denial of Death*—alongside the more "cosmological"
schemes of Aquinas.[23] Moreover, it is a hoax to limit Aquinas'
enterprise to accounting for the natural world, as *we* are prone
to conceive it. For the third way "is based on what need not be
and on what must be," the fourth "on the gradation observed
in things," and the fifth "on the guidedness of nature." Here
we are dealing, as many critics have reminded us, not with
"nature itself" so much as with the characteristic ways we
have of understanding it. Once this has been remarked, the first
and second ways—"based on change" and "on the nature of
causation"—appear to answer to the same general concerns.

The point of the "proofs," then, would be to show how one's
more general explanatory schemes fail to met their originating
intention. The "proofs" try to accomplish this aim by making
one aware of the *shape* of those questions which do shape our
inquiry into nature (including ourselves), but do not admit of
determinate answer. I spoke of these earlier as the parameters
of human existence: our origins, our degree of participation
in continuing that mode of existence, and our individual (and
collective) destinies. If these questions become painfully conscious regarding human existence, they are not unconnected
with our quest for understanding the rest of nature as well. In
fact, our tendency to conceive nature and history as logically
independent domains seems to be ingredient in our relative
incapacity to think ecologically.[24]

To become aware of the shape of such shaping questions is not to produce a god, certainly, but it is to learn how to find one's way in those regions where the existence or non-existence of God would make a difference. To determine what difference that could be, and to learn how to assess the consequences, would be one of the ways in which a person would come to or eschew the affirmation of God.

The reasons why one must speak so formally and indirectly here are theological. To be divine, God's action cannot appear in a determinate fashion. As Aquinas puts it, the proper effect of God's action is that something exist, and *to exist* is not a feature. So we will not be able to turn God up as an object, nor identify any proper effect of divinity. That is a grammatical observation.

So the truth of affirmations about divinity—notably that God is present to us—would best be forced upon one as a radical presupposition or ground for acting. And not for just any kind of activity, but for that unique activity of becoming who I am. It is difficult to say, of course, how affirmations about divinity can play the role of grounding that becoming; yet one can show that this is precisely the task which such affirmations are designed to perform. Again, the enterprise of "proving God's existence" could occupy itself with examining candidates for the role which grounds self-becoming, and in the process come somewhat clearer about that role. The point of such activity would be to prepare one to recognize how God works in a life, even if one could never identify certain actions as divine.

The response to God at work in a life is, of course, faith; so a "proof" will be successful in the measure that it functions to justify our believing. So the parallel drawn between "proofs" and justification proves to be more than a strategic one. A successful proof turns out to be an activity which succeeds in justifying religious belief. Yet in the process, our ordinary conceptions of both activities have been made over. That is the sort of thing which happens, I believe, when one begins to engage in the activity of "proving" God's existence. They are not proofs, then, so much as performances, since they do not arrive at a conclusion so much as engage those who pursue them in a quest for the shape of the questions which shape our lives and hence serve as parameters for inquiry into the universe. In the measure that such questioning is presupposed to any determinate human inquiry, the logical neighborhood of originating power or divinity has been located. Were a proof to "turn something up" there, however, it would not be God, for divinity cannot be turned up, though it may present itself. What the activity should have prepared us to do, however, is to discriminate among the various contenders for divinity, and that skill should assist us in identifying authentic paths to God.

NOTES

1. Aquinas, *Summa Theologiae* 1.2, Intro. All references to Aquinas will be to the Eyre and Spottiswoode/McGraw-Hill edition, notably to Volume 2: *Existence and Nature of God*, trans. T. McDermott, O.P. (1964) [containing 1.2-11] and to Volume 3: *Knowing and Naming God*, trans. H. McCabe, O.P. (1964) [1.12-13].

2. *Summa Theologiae* 1.2.3: "Dicendum quod Deum esse quinque viis *probari* potest."

3. Cf. C. K. Grant, "Pragmatic Implication," *Philosophy* 33 (1958), 303-24, and P. F. Strawson, *Introduction to Logical Theory* (New York, 1952), on "presupposition," pp. 175-79.

4. Cf. my *Exercises in Religious Understanding* (Notre Dame, Ind., 1974) chap. 1: "Augustine: Understanding as a Personal Quest;" and W. O'Brien, "On Teaching Augustine's *Confessions*," *Horizons* 5 (1978), 47-62.

5. St. Anselm's *Proslogion*, trans. M. J. Charlesworth (Oxford, 1965; Notre Dame, Ind., 1979), Preface, p. 103.

6. The verbal distinction between "nominal" and "real" definitions is (so far as I know) later than Anselm, but Anselm's way of proceeding shows that the project itself was clear to him. For a summary description of this distinction, see my *Analogy and Philosophical Language* (New Haven, Conn., 1973).

7. Charlesworth's *excursus* on Karl Barth's *Fides Quaerens Intellectum* (New York, 1960) displays how someone steeped in medieval thought can handle a reading like Barth's: "To sum up: if Barth's interpretation of St. Anselm's position on faith and reason is correct, St. Anselm must have been out of step with the whole Augustinian tradition of his own time" (p. 45—see entire section pp. 40-45).

8. It is difficult to know whether Anselm had access to this very work, but the substance of Aristotle's logical treatises was available in the eleventh century.

9. Cf. my *Exercises*, chap. 2: "Anselm: Formulating the Quest for Understanding."

10. *Summa Theologiae* 1.3.4: "Sua . . . essentia est suum esse."

11. I have sketched out this interpretation of Aquinas' "doctrine of God" in *Exercises in Religious Understanding*, chap. 3, and defended it at length in *Aquinas: God and Action* (Notre Dame, Ind., 1979). I present the formula "to be God is to be" as a summary expression of Aquinas' criterion of simpleness. More exactly, it should be read "[to be] God is [to be] to be."

12. I am indebted to Victor Preller for this analysis: *Divine Science and the Science of God* (Princeton, N.J., 1967), pp. 109–35, esp. pp. 135, 155.

13. Norman Kemp Smith, trans., *Immanuel Kant's Critique of Pure Reason* (London, 1961), pp. 532-70.

14. Joel Feinberg, "Noncomparative Justice," in J. Feinberg and H. Gross, eds., *Justice* (Belmont, Cal., 1977), p. 60.

15. Cf. note 3.

16. Alastair McKinnon, *Falsification and Belief* (The Hague, 1970), pp. 23–46, reprinted by Ridgeview, Reseda, Cal., 1978.

17. McKinnon's objections to the device of analogy (p. 52) have been met by my extended discussion in *Analogy*. His recourse to "heuristic" expressions corresponds nicely with classical uses of analogous terms.

18. *Summa Theologiae* 1.47.1, 2-1.91.2.

19. For a careful analysis of *convictions* and their cognitive status, see James McClendon and James Smith, *Understanding Religious Convictions* (Notre Dame, Ind., 1975).

20. Brian Wicker's fascinating essay. *The Story-Shaped World* (Notre Dame, Ind., 1975) offers different perspectives on the cognitive role of stories.

21. Cf. Alisdair MacIntyre, "Epistemological Crises, Dramatic Narrative and the Philosophy of Science," *Monist* 60 (1977), 453–72.

22. Patrick Sherry, "Philosophy and the Saints," *Heythrop Journal* 8 (1977), 23-37.

23. Ernest Becker, *Denial of Death* (New York, 1974).

24. Peter Winch, "Understanding a Primitive Society," in Bryan Wilson, ed., *Rationality* (Oxford, 1970) pp. 78-111.

Moral Arguments for Theistic Belief

ROBERT MERRIHEW ADAMS

Moral arguments were the type of theistic argument most characteristic of the nineteenth and early twentieth centuries. More recently they have become one of philosophy's abandoned farms. The fields are still fertile, but they have not been cultivated systematically since the latest methods came in. The rambling Victorian farmhouse has not been kept up as well as similar structures, and people have not been stripping the sentimental gingerbread off the porches to reveal the clean lines of argument. This paper is intended to contribute to the remedy of this neglect. It will deal with quite a number of arguments, because I think we can understand them better if we place them in relation to each other. This will not leave time to be as subtle, historically or philosophically, as I would like to be, but I hope I will be able to prove something more than my own taste for Victoriana.

I ⎯⎯⎯

Let us begin with one of the most obvious, though perhaps never the most fashionable, arguments on the farm: an Argument from the Nature of Right and Wrong. We believe quite firmly that certain things are morally right and others are morally wrong—for example, that it is wrong to torture another person to death just for fun. Questions may be raised about the nature of that which is believed in these beliefs: what does the rightness or wrongness of an act consist in? I believe that the most adequate answer is provided by a theory that entails the existence of God—specifically, by the theory that moral rightness and wrongness consist in agreement and disagreement, respectively, with the will or commands of a loving God. One of the most generally accepted reasons for believing in the existence of anything is that its existence is implied by the theory that seems to account most adequately for some subject matter. I take it, therefore, that my metaethical views provide me with a reason of some weight for believing in the existence of God.

Perhaps some will think it disreputably "tender-minded" to accept such a reason where the subject matter is moral. It may be suggested that the epistemological status of moral beliefs is so far inferior to that of physical beliefs, for example, that any moral belief found to entail the existence of an otherwise unknown object ought simply to be abandoned. But in spite of the general uneasiness about morality that pervades our culture, most of us do hold many moral beliefs with almost the highest degree of confidence. So long as we think it reasonable to argue at all from grounds that are not absolutely certain, there is no clear reason why such confident beliefs, in ethics as in other fields, should not be accepted as premises in arguing for the existence of anything that is required for the most satisfactory theory of their subject matter.[1]

The divine command theory of the nature of right and wrong combines two advantages not jointly possessed by any of its non-theological competitors. These advantages are sufficiently obvious that their nature can be indicated quite briefly to persons familiar with the metaethical debate, though they are also so controversial that it would take a book-length review of the contending theories to defend my claims. The first advantage of divine command metaethics is that it presents facts of moral rightness and wrongness as objective, non-natural facts—objective in the sense that whether they obtain or not does not depend on whether any human being thinks they do; and non-natural in the sense that they cannot be stated entirely in the language of physics, chemistry, biology, and human or animal psychology. For it is an objective but not a natural fact that God commands, permits, or forbids something. Intuitively this is an advantage. If we are tempted to say that there are only natural facts of right and wrong, or that there are no objective facts of right and wrong at all, it is chiefly because we have found so much obscurity in theories about objective, non-natural ethical facts. We seem not to be acquainted with the simple, non-natural ethical properties of the Intuitionists, and we do not understand what a Platonic Form of the Good or the Just would be. The second advantage of divine command metaethics is that it is relatively intelligible. There are certainly difficulties in the notion of a divine command, but at least it provides us more clearly with matter for thought than the Intuitionist and Platonic conceptions do.

We need not discuss here to what extent these advantages of the divine command theory may be possessed by other theological metaethical theories—for example, by views according to which moral principles do not depend on God's will for their validity, but on His understanding for their ontological status. Such theories, if one is inclined to accept them, can of course be made the basis of an argument for theism.[2]

What we cannot avoid discussing, and at greater length than the advantages, are the alleged disadvantages of divine command metaethics. The advantages may be easily recognized, but the disadvantages are generally thought to be decisive. I have argued elsewhere, in some detail, that they are not decisive.[3] Here let us concentrate on three objections that are particularly important for the present argument.

(1) In accordance with the conception of metaethics as analysis of the meanings of terms, a divine command theory is often construed as claiming that 'right' *means* commanded (or permitted) by God, and that 'wrong' *means* forbidden by God. This gives rise to the objection that people who do not believe that there exists a God to command or forbid still use the terms 'right' and 'wrong', and are said (even by theists) to believe that certain actions are right and others wrong. Surely those atheists do not mean by 'right' and 'wrong' what the divine command theory seems to say they must mean. Moreover, it may be objected that any argument for the existence of God from the

premise that certain actions are right and others wrong will be viciously circular if that premise *means* that certain actions are commanded or permitted by God and others forbidden by God.

One might reply that it is not obviously impossible for someone to disbelieve something that is analytically implied by something else that he asserts. Nor is it impossible for the conclusion of a perfectly good, non-circular argument to be analytically implied by its premises. But issues about the nature of conceptual analysis, and of circularity in argument, can be avoided here. For in the present argument, a divine command theory need not be construed as saying that the existence of God is analytically implied by ascriptions of rightness and wrongness. It can be construed as proposing an answer to a question left open by the meaning of "right" and "wrong," rather than as a theory of the meaning of those terms.

The ordinary meanings of many terms that signify properties, such as 'hot' and 'electrically charged', do not contain enough information to answer all questions about the nature (or even in some cases the identity) of the properties signified. Analysis of the meaning of 'wrong' might show, for example, that 'Nuclear deterrence is wrong' ascribes to nuclear deterrence a property about which the speaker may be certain of very little except that it belongs, independently of his views, to many actions that he opposes, such as torturing people just for fun. The analysis of meaning need not completely determine the identity of this property, but it may still be argued that a divine command theory identifies it most adequately.

(2) The gravest objection to the more extreme forms of divine command theory is that they imply that if God commanded us, for example, to make it our chief end in life to inflict suffering on other human beings, for no other reason than that He commanded it, it would be *wrong* not to obey. Finding this conclusion unacceptable, I prefer a less extreme, or modified, divine command theory, which identifies the ethical property of wrongness with the property of being contrary to the commands of a *loving* God. Since a God who commanded us to practice cruelty for its own sake would not be a loving God, this modified divine command theory does not imply that it would be wrong to disobey such a command.

But the objector may continue his attack: "Suppose that God did not exist, or that He existed but did not love us. Even the modified divine command theory implies that in that case it would not be wrong to be cruel to other people. But surely it would be wrong."

The objector may have failed to distinguish sharply two claims he may want to make: that some acts *would* be wrong even if God *did* not exist, and that some acts *are* wrong even if God *does* not exist. I grant the latter. Even if divine command metaethics is the best theory of the nature of right and wrong, there are other theories which are more plausible than denying that cruelty is wrong. If God does not exist, my theory is false; but presumably the best alternative to it is true, and cruelty is still wrong.

But suppose there is in fact a God—indeed a loving God— and that the ethical property of wrongness is the property of being forbidden by a loving God. It follows that no actions would be wrong in a world in which no loving God existed, if 'wrong' designates rigidly (that is, in every possible world) the property that it actually designates.[4] For no actions would have that property in such a world. Even in a world without God, however, the best remaining alternative to divine command metaethics might be correct in the following way. In such a world there could be people very like us who would say truly, "Kindness is right," and "Cruelty is wrong." They would be speaking about kindness and cruelty, but not about rightness and wrongness. That is, they would not be speaking about the properties that *are* rightness and wrongness, though they might be speaking about properties (perhaps natural properties) that they would be *calling* 'rightness' and 'wrongness.' But they would be using the words 'right' and 'wrong' with the same *meaning* as we actually do. For the meaning of the words, I assume, leaves open some questions about the identity of the properties they designate.

Some divine command theorists could not consistently reply as I have suggested to the present objection. Their theory is about the meaning of 'right' and 'wrong', or they think all alternatives to it (except the complete denial of moral distinctions) are too absurd to play the role I have suggested for alternative theories. But there is another reply that is open to them. They can say that although wrongness is not a property that would be possessed by cruelty in a world without God, the possibility or idea of cruelty-in-a-world-without-God *does* possess, in the actual world (with God), a property that is close kin to wrongness: the property of being frowned on, or viewed with disfavor, by God. The experience of responding emotionally to fiction should convince us that it is possible to view with the strongest favor or disfavor events regarded as taking place in a world that would not, or might not, include one's own existence—and if possible for us, why not for God? If we are inclined to say that cruelty in a world without God would be wrong, that is surely because of an attitude of disfavor that we have in the actual world toward such a possibility. And if our attitude corresponds to an objective, non-natural moral fact, why cannot that fact be one that obtains in the actual world, rather than in the supposed world without God?

(3) It may be objected that the advantages of the divine command theory can be obtained without an entailment of God's existence. For the rightness of an action might be said to consist in the fact that the action *would* agree with the commands of a loving God if one existed, *or* does so agree if a loving God exists. This modification transforms the divine command theory into a non-naturalistic form of the ideal observer theory of the nature of right and wrong.[5] It has the advantage of identifying rightness and wrongness with properties that actions could have even if God does not exist. And of course it takes away the basis of my metaethical argument for theism.

The flaw in this theory is that it is difficult to see what is supposed to be the force of the counterfactual conditional that is centrally involved in it. If there is no loving God, what makes it the case if there were one, He would command this rather than that? Without an answer to this question, the crucial counterfactual lacks a clear sense. I can see only two possible answers: either that what any possible loving God would command is logically determined by the concept of a loving God, or that it is determined by a causal law. Neither answer seems likely to work without depriving the theory of some part of the advantages of divine command metaethics.

No doubt some conclusions about what He would not command follow *logically* or analytically from the concept of a loving God. He would not command us to practice cruelty for its own sake, for example. But in some cases, at least, in which we believe the act is wrong, it seems only contingent that a loving God does or would frown on increasing the happiness of other people by the painless and undetected killing of a person who wants to live but will almost certainly not live happily.[6] Very diverse preferences about what things are to be treated as personal rights seem compatible with love and certainly with deity. Of course, you could explicitly build all your moral principles into the definition of the kind of hypothetical divine commands that you take to make facts of right and wrong. But then the fact that your principles *would* be endorsed by the commands of such a God adds nothing to the principles themselves; whereas endorsement by an *actual* divine command would add something, which is one of the advantages of divine command metaethics.

Nor is it plausible to suppose that there are *causal* laws that determine what would be commanded by a loving God, if there is no God. All causal laws, at bottom, are about actual things. There are no causal laws, though there could be legends, about the metabolism of chimeras or the susceptibility of centaurs to polio. There are physical laws about frictionless motions which never occur, but they are extrapolated from facts about actual motions. And we can hardly obtain a causal law about the commands of a possible loving God by extrapolating from causal laws governing the behavior of monkeys, chimpanzees, and human beings, as if every possible God would simply be a very superior primate. Any such extrapolation, moreover, would destroy the character of the theory of hypothetical divine commands as a theory of *non-natural* facts.

Our discussion of the Argument from the Nature of Right and Wrong may be concluded with some reflections on the nature of the God in whose existence it gives us some reason to believe. (1) The appeal of the argument lies in the provision of an explanation of moral facts of whose truth we are already confident. It must therefore be taken as an argument for the existence of a God whose commands—and presumably, whose purposes and character as well—are in accord with our most confident judgments of right and wrong. I have suggested that He must be a loving God. (2) He must be an intelligent being, so that it makes sense to speak of His having a will and issuing commands. Maximum adequacy of a divine command theory surely requires that God be supposed to have enormous knowledge and understanding of ethically relevant facts, if not absolute omniscience. He should be a God "unto whom all hearts are open, all desires known, and from whom no secrets are hid." (3) The argument does not seem to imply very much about God's power, however—certainly not that He is omnipotent. (4) Nor is it obvious that the argument supports belief in the unity or uniqueness of God. Maybe the metaethical place of divine commands could be taken by the unanimous deliverances of a senate of deities—although that conception raises troublesome questions about the nature of the morality or quasi-morality that must govern the relations of the gods with each other.

II

The most influential moral arguments for theistic belief have been a family of arguments that may be called Kantian. They have a common center in the idea of a moral order of the universe and are arguments for belief in a God sufficiently powerful to establish and maintain such an order. The Kantian family has members on both sides of one of the most fundamental distinctions in this area—the distinction between *theoretical* and *practical* arguments. By "a theoretical moral argument for theistic belief" I mean an argument having an ethical premise and purporting to prove the *truth*, or enhance the *probability*, of theism. By "a practical argument for theistic belief" I mean an argument purporting only to give ethical or other practical reasons for *believing* that God exists. The practical argument may have no direct bearing at all on the truth or probability of the belief whose practical advantage it extols.

Arguments from the Nature of Right and Wrong are clearly theoretical moral arguments for theistic belief. Kant, without warning us of any such distinction, gives us sometimes a theoretical and sometimes a practical argument (in my sense of "theoretical" and "practical," not his). His theoretical argument goes roughly as follows:

> (A) We ought (morally) to promote the realization of the highest good.
> (B) What we ought to do must be possible for us to do.
> (C) It is not possible for us to promote the realization of the highest good unless there exists a God who makes the realization possible.
> (D) Therefore, there exists such a God.

Kant was not clear about the theoretical character of this argument, and stated as its conclusion that "it is morally necessary to *assume* the existence of God."[7] Its premises, however, plainly imply the more theoretical conclusion that God exists.

(C) needs explanation. Kant conceived of the highest good as composed of two elements. The first element, moral virtue, depends on the wills of moral agents and does not require divine intervention for its possibility. But the second element, the happiness of moral agents in strict proportion to their virtue, will not be realized unless there is a moral order of the universe. Such an order, Kant argues, cannot be expected of the laws of nature, without God.

Doubts may be raised whether Kant's conception of the highest good is ethically correct and whether there might not be some non-theistic basis for a perfect proportionment of happiness to virtue. But a more decisive objection has often been made to (A): in any reasonable morality we will be obligated to promote only the best attainable approximation of the highest good. For this reason Kant's theoretical moral argument for theism does not seem very promising to me.[8]

Elsewhere Kant argues quite differently. He even denies that a command to promote the highest good is contained in, or analytically derivable from, the moral law. He claims rather that we will be "hindered" from doing what the moral law commands us to do unless we can regard our actions as contributing to the realization of "a final end of all things" which we can also make a "final end for all our actions and abstentions." He argues that only the highest good can serve morally as such a final end and that we therefore have a compelling moral need to believe in the possibility of its realization.[9] This yields only a practical argument for theistic belief. Stripped of some of its more distinctively Kantian dress, it can be stated in terms of "demoralization," by which I mean a weakening or deterioration of moral motivation.

(E) It would be demoralizing not to believe there is a moral order of the universe; for then we would have to regard it as very likely that the history of the universe will not be good on the whole, no matter what we do.

(F) Demoralization is morally undesirable.

(G) Therefore, there is moral advantage in believing that there is a moral order of the universe.

(H) Theism provides the most adequate theory of a moral order of the universe.

(J) Therefore, there is a moral advantage in accepting theism.

What is a moral order of the universe? I shall not formulate any necessary condition. But let us say that the following is *logically sufficient* for the universe's having a moral order: (1) a good world-history requires something besides human virtue (it might, as Kant thought, require the happiness of the virtuous); but (2) the universe is such that morally good actions will probably contribute to a good world-history. (I use 'world' as a convenient synonym for 'universe'.)

Theism has several secular competitors as a theory of a moral order of the universe in this sense. The idea of scientific and cultural progress has provided liberal thinkers, and Marxism has provided socialists, with hopes of a good world-history without God. It would be rash to attempt to adjudicate this competition here. I shall therefore not comment further on the truth of (H) but concentrate on the argument from (E) and (F) to (G). It is, after all, of great interest in itself, religiously and in other ways, if morality gives us a reason to believe in a moral order of the universe.

Is (E) true? Would it indeed be demoralizing not to believe there is a moral order of the universe? The issue is in large part empirical. It is for sociologists and psychologists to investigate scientifically what are the effects of various beliefs on human motivation. And the motivational effects of religious belief form one of the central themes of the classics of speculative sociology.[10] But I have the impression that there has not yet been very much "hard" empirical research casting light directly on the question whether (E) is true.

It may be particularly difficult to develop empirical research techniques subtle enough philosophically to produce results relevant to our present argument. One would have to specify which phenomena count as a weakening or deterioration of moral motivation. One would also have to distinguish the effects of belief in a moral world-order from the effects of other religious beliefs, for (E) could be true even if, as some have held, the effects of actual religious beliefs have been predominantly bad from a moral point of view. The bad consequences might be due to doctrines which are separable from faith in a moral order of the universe.

Lacking scientifically established answers to the empirical aspects of our question, we may say, provisionally, what seems plausible to us. And (E) does seem quite plausible to me. Seeing our lives as contributing to a valued larger whole is one of the things that gives them a point in our own eyes. The morally good person cares about the goodness of what happens in the world and not just about the goodness of his own actions. If a right action can be seen as contributing to some great good, that increases the importance it has for him. Conversely, if he thinks that things will turn out badly no matter what he does, and especially if he thinks that (as often appears to be the case) the long-range effects of right action are about as likely to be bad as good,[11] that will diminish the emotional attraction that duty exerts on him.[12] Having to regard it as very likely that the history of the universe will not be good on the whole, no matter what one does, seems apt to induce a cynical sense of futility about the moral life, undermining one's moral resolve and one's interest in moral considerations. My judgment on this issue is subject to two qualifications, however.

(1) We cannot plausibly ascribe more than a demoralizing *tendency* to disbelief in a moral order of the universe. There are certainly people who do not believe in such an order, but show no signs of demoralization.

(2) It may be doubted how much most people are affected by beliefs or expectations about the history of the universe as a whole. Perhaps most of us could sustain with comparative equanimity the bleakest of pessimism about the twenty-third century if only we held brighter hopes for the nearer future of our own culture, country, or family, or even (God forgive us!) our own philosophy department. The belief that we can accomplish something significant and good for our own immediate collectivities may be quite enough to keep us going morally. On the other hand, belief in a larger-scale moral order of the universe might be an important bulwark against demoralization if all or most of one's more immediate hopes were being dashed. I doubt that there has ever been a time when moralists could afford to ignore questions about the motivational resources available in such desperate situations. Certainly it would be unimaginative to suppose that we live in such a time.

Some will object that those with the finest moral motivation can find all the inspiration they need in a tragic beauty of the moral life itself, even if they despair about the course of history. The most persuasive argument for this view is a presentation that succeeds in evoking moral emotion in connection with the thought of tragedy; Bertrand Russell's early essay "A Free Man's Worship"[13] is an eloquent example. But I remain somewhat skeptical. Regarded aesthetically, from the outside, tragedy may be sublimely beautiful; lived from the inside, over a long period of time, I fear it is only too likely to end in discouragement and bitterness, though no doubt there have been shining exceptions.

But the main objection to the present argument is an objection to all practical arguments. It is claimed that none of them give justifying reasons for believing anything at all. If there are any practical advantages that are worthy to sway us in accepting or rejecting a belief, the advantage of not being demoralized is surely one of them. But can it be right, and intellectually honest, to believe something, or try to believe it, for the sake of any practical advantage, however noble?

I believe it can. This favorable verdict on practical arguments for theoretical conclusions is particularly plausible in "cases where faith creates its own verification," as William James puts it[14]—or where your wish is at least more likely to come true if you believe it will. Suppose you are running for Congress and an unexpected misfortune has made it doubtful whether you still have a good chance of winning. Probably it will at least be clear that you are more likely to win if you continue to believe that your chances are good. Believing will keep up your spirits and your alertness, boost the morale of your campaign workers, and make other people more likely to take you seriously. In this case it seems to me eminently reasonable for you to cling, for the sake of practical advantage, to the belief that you have a good chance of winning.

Another type of belief for which practical arguments can seem particularly compelling is trust in a person. Suppose a close friend of mine is accused of a serious crime. I know him well and can hardly believe he would do such a thing. He insists he is innocent. But the evidence against him, though not conclusive, is very strong. So far as I can judge the total evidence (including my knowledge of his character) in a cool, detached way, I would have to say it is quite evenly balanced. I want to believe in his innocence, and there is reason to think that I ought, morally, to believe in it if I can. For he may well be innocent. If he is, he will have a deep psychological need for someone to believe him. If no one believes him, he will suffer unjustly a loneliness perhaps greater than the loneliness of guilt. And who will believe him if his close friends do not? Who will believe him if I do not? Of course I could try to *pretend* to believe him. If I do that I will certainly be less honest with him, and I doubt that I will be more honest with myself, than if

I really cling to the belief that he is innocent. Moreover, the pretense is unlikely to satisfy his need to be believed. If he knows me well and sees me often, my insincerity will probably betray itself to him in some spontaneous reaction.

The legitimacy of practical arguments must obviously be subject to some restrictions. Two important restrictions were suggested by William James. (1) Practical arguments should be employed only on questions that "cannot . . . be decided on intellectual grounds."[15] There should be a plurality of alternatives that one finds intellectually plausible. (The option should be "living," as James would put it.) Faith ought not to be "believing what you know ain't so." It also ought not to short-circuit rational inquiry; we ought not to try to settle by practical argument an issue that we could settle by further investigation of evidence in the time available for settling it. (2) The question to be decided by practical argument should be urgent and of practical importance ("forced" and "momentous," James would say). If it can wait or is pragmatically inconsequential, we can afford to suspend judgment about it; and it is healthier to do so.

To these I would add a third important restriction: it would be irrational to accept a belief on the ground that it gives you a *reason* for doing something that you want to do. To the extent that your belief is based on a desire to do x, it cannot add to your reasons for doing x. There will be a vicious practical circle in a practical argument for any belief unless it is judged that the belief would be advantageous even if it were no more probable than it seems to be in advance of the practical argument. It may be rational to be swayed by a practical argument, on the other hand, if one is not inventing a reason for doing something, but trying to sustain in oneself the emotional conditions for doing something one already has enough reason to want to do.

Suppose again that you are a congressional candidate trying, for practical reasons, to maintain in yourself the belief that you have a good chance to win. This is irrational if your aim is to get yourself to do things that you think it would be unreasonable to do if you were less confident. But it is not irrational if your primary aim is to foster in yourself the right spirit to do most effectively things you think it reasonable to do anyway. The rationality of your trying, for practical reasons, to believe depends in this case on the strengths of your antecedent commitment to going all out to win the election.

Similarly I think that the rationality of trying for moral reasons to believe in a moral order of the universe depends in large measure on the antecedent strength of one's commitment to morality. If one is strongly committed, so that one wishes to be moral even if the world is not, and if one seeks, not reasons to be moral, but emotional undergirding for the moral life, then it may well be rational to be swayed by the practical argument for the belief.

It can also be intellectually honest, provided that one acknowledges to oneself the partly voluntary character and practical basis of one's belief. In speaking of honesty here, what I have in mind is that there is no self-deception going on, and that one is forming one's belief in accordance with principles that one approves and would commend in other cases.

But there are other intellectual virtues besides honesty.[16] It is an intellectual virtue to proportion the strength of one's belief to the strength of the evidence in most cases.[17] On the other hand, it seems to be an intellectual virtue, and is surely not a vice, to think charitably of other people. And what is it to think charitably of others? It is, in part, to require less evidence to think well of them than to think ill of them, and thus, in some cases, not to proportion the strength of one's belief to the strength of the evidence. Yet thinking charitably of others is not a species of intellectual dishonesty. Neither is it invariably an intellectual vice to be swayed by practical arguments.

III

Both Kantian and Christian theism imply that true self-interest is in harmony with morality. Kant believed that in the long run one's happiness will be strictly proportioned to one's virtue. And if that would be denied by many Christian theologians for the sake of the doctrine of grace, they would at least maintain that no one can enjoy the greatest happiness without a deep moral commitment and that every good person will be very happy in the long run. They believe that the most important parts of a good person's self-interest are eternally *safe*, no matter how much his virtue or saintliness may lead him to sacrifice here below. The truth of these beliefs is surely another logically sufficient condition of the universe's having a moral order. (I assume that virtue is not so richly its own reward as to be sufficient in itself for happiness.)

There are both theoretical and practical arguments for theistic belief which are first of all arguments for faith in a moral world-order that harmonizes self-interest with morality. As such, they belong to the Kantian type. For obvious reasons, let us call them "individualistic," by contrast with Kant's own, more "universalistic," arguments.

The practical arguments of this individualistic Kantian type depend on the claim that it would be demoralizing not to believe in a harmony of self-interest with virtue. Many religious and social thinkers, from Greek antiquity to Freud,[18] have ascribed to the gods the function of invisible policemen, reinforcing moral motivation with self-concern, through belief in supernatural rewards and punishments. Disbelief in this cosmic constabulary has been widely feared as a breach in the dike that holds back our baser desires. It is doubtful, however, that the gods have been effective policemen. One of the few relatively "hard" empirical data in this area is that criminal behavior is not negatively correlated with assent to religious doctrines.[19]

For this reason I think we are likely to obtain a more plausible argument for the moral advantage of belief in a harmony of self-interest with virtue if we focus not on gross but on subtle demoralization—not on the avoidance of crime but on the higher reaches of the moral life.[20] The conviction that every good person will be very happy in the long run has often contributed, in religious believers, to a cheerfulness and single-heartedness of moral devotion that they probably would not have had without it. This integration of motives may be regarded as morally advantageous even if its loss does not lead to criminality.

I anticipate the objection that self-interest has no place in the highest ethical motives, and that belief in the harmony of self-interest with morality therefore debases rather than elevates one's motivation. What could be nobler than the virtuous sacrifice of what one regards as one's only chance for great happiness? Yet such sacrifice is rendered impossible by faith in the sure reward of virtue.

I have two replies. (1) Self-interest remains a powerful motive in the best of us; a life of which that was not true would hardly be recognizable as human. It is not obvious that a hard-won victory over even the most enlightened self-interest is morally preferable to the integration of motives resulting from the belief that it will be well with the righteous in the long run. Those who hold that belief still have plenty of victories to win over shorter-sighted desires. And it is plausible to suppose—though I do not know that anyone has proved it—that we are *more likely* to attain to the goodness that is possible through an integration of motives, than to win a death-struggle with our own deepest self-interest, since the latter is so hard.

(2) It is not only in our own case that we have to be concerned about the relation between self-interest and virtue. We influence the actions of other people and particularly of people we love. Morally, no doubt, we ought to influence them in the direction of always doing right (so far as it is appropriate to influence them deliberately at all). But as we care about their self-interest too, our encouragement of virtue in them is apt to be more wholehearted and therefore more effective, if we believe that they will be happy in the long run if they do right.[21] It is hard to see any ground for a charge of selfishness in this aspect of faith in the sure reward of virtue. It is not unambiguously noble (though it might be right) to encourage someone else—even someone you love—to make a great and permanent sacrifice of his true self-interest. We have no reason to regret the loss of opportunities to influence others so sadly.

I am more disturbed by another objection. I have said that it is irrational to accept a belief on the ground that it gives you a *reason* for doing something. Someone may, of course, seriously and reflectively want to live always as he morally ought, even if doing so really costs him his only chance at happiness. He may therefore already have reason enough to resist cowardice, weakness of will, and any grudging attitude toward his duty. And he may correctly judge that thinking of his happiness as assured in the long run (in a life after death, if necessary) would provide *emotional* strength against such temptations. Only in such a case may one reasonably be swayed by a practical argument for faith in a harmony of self-interest with virtue. But this faith—much more than faith in the possiblity of a good world-history—seems perilously likely to be regarded as morally advantageous chiefly on the fraudulent ground that it gives one a reason for living virtuously, or perhaps takes away reasons for not living virtuously. Indeed, where it is our encouragement of *other* people's virtue that is at issue, it seems doubtful that we *ought* to seek comfort or fortitude in anything but reasons. There is no particular virtue in my *feeling* better about the sacrifices I encourage you to make.

This interest in reasons for being moral, which threatens to vitiate a practical argument, forms the basis of an interesting theoretical moral argument for a harmony of self-interest with morality.[22] It is widely thought that moral judgments have an action- and preference-guiding force that they could not have unless everyone had reason to follow them in his actions and preferences. But there has also been widespread dissatisfaction with arguments purporting to show that everyone does have reason always to be moral. It has even been suggested that this dissatisfaction ought to lead us to moderate the claims we have been accustomed to make for the force of the moral "ought."[23]

It is plausibly assumed, however, that virtually everyone has a deep and strong desire for his own happiness. So if happiness will in the long run be strictly proportioned to moral goodness, that explains how virtually everyone does have an important reason to want to be good. We may fairly count this as a theoretical advantage of Kantian theism, if we are intuitively inclined to believe that moral judgments have a force that implies that virtually everyone has reason to follow them.

This advantage of Kantian theism may be shared by other, perhaps more Christian theologies in which the connection between happiness and virtue is less strict, provided they imply (as I would expect them to) that everyone would be very happy, and more satisfied with his life, in the long run, if he lived always as he morally and religiously ought. The advantage is certainly shared by some non-theistic theories. The Buddhist doctrine of Karma is instanced by Sidgwick as a theory of "rewards inseparably attaching to right conduct . . . by the natural operation of an impersonal Law."[24] I think it is plausible, however, to suppose that if we are to have such a harmony of self-interest with duty, we must have recourse to the supernatural and presumably to an enormously powerful and knowledgeable virtuous agent.

I doubt that this line of argument can provide a really strong support for any sort of theism. For on the basis of intuitive appeal, the premise that moral judgments have a force that implies that virtually everyone has reason to follow them will not bear nearly as much weight as the conviction that some acts are morally right and others wrong, which served as a premise in my Argument from the Nature of Right and Wrong.

I have focused, as most philosphical discussion of the moral arguments has, on the connections of theism with the nature of right and wrong and with the idea of a moral order of the universe. I am keenly aware that they form only part of the total moral case for theistic belief. Theistic conceptions of guilt and forgiveness,[25] for example, or of God as a friend who witnesses, judges, appreciates, and can remember all of our actions, choices, and emotions, may well have theoretical and practical moral advantages at least as compelling as any that we have discussed.

IV

Perhaps moral arguments establish at most subsidiary advantages of belief in God's existence. They are more crucial to the case for His goodness. Causal arguments, in particular, from the existence and qualities of the world, may have some force to persuade us that there is a God; but they plainly have much less support to offer the proposition,

(K) If there is a God, He is morally very good.

(Here I define 'a God' as a creator and governor of the whole universe, supreme in understanding and knowledge as well as in power, so that (K) is not a tautology.)

There is a powerful moral argument for (K). Belief in the existence of an evil or amoral God would be morally intolerable. In view of His power, such belief would be apt to carry with it all the disadvantages, theoretical and practical, of disbelief in a moral order of the universe. But I am even more concerned about the consequences it would have in view of His knowledge and understanding. We are to think of a being who understands human life much better than we do—understands it well enough to create and control it. Among other things, He must surely understand our moral ideas and feelings. He understands everyone's point of view, and has a more objective, or at least a more complete and balanced view of human relationships than any of us can have. He has whatever self-control, stability, and integration of purpose are implied in His having produced a world as constant in its causal order as our own. And now we are to suppose that that being does not care to support with His will the moral principles that we believe are true. We are to suppose that He either opposes some of them, or does not care enough about some of them to act on them. I submit that if we really believed there is a God like that, who understands so much and yet disregards some or all of our moral principles, it would be extremely difficult for us to continue to regard those principles with the respect that we believe is due them. Since we believe that we ought to pay them that respect, this is a great moral disadvantage of the belief that there is an evil or amoral God.

I think the same disadvantage attends even the belief that there is a morally slack God, since moral slackness involves some disregard of moral principles. There might seem to be less danger in the belief that there is a morally weak God—perhaps one who can't resist the impulse to toy with us immorally, but who feels guilty about it. At least He would be seen as caring enough about moral principles to feel guilty. But He would not be seen as caring enough about them to control a childish impulse. And I think that our respect for the moral law will be undermined by any belief which implies that our moral sensibilities were created, and are thoroughly understood, by a being who does not find an absolutely controlling importance in the ends and principles of true morality.

I shall not offer here a definitive answer to the question, whether this moral argument for belief in God's goodness is theoretical or practical. There may be metaethical views— perhaps some ideal observer theory—which imply that nothing could be a true moral principle if there is a God who does not fully accept it. Such views, together with the thesis that there are true moral principles, would imply the truth of (K) and not merely the desirability of believing (K). That would produce a theoretical argument.

On the other hand, it might be claimed that moral principles would still be true, and the respect that is due them undiminished, if there were an evil or amoral God, but that it would be psychologically difficult or impossible for us to respect them as we ought if we believed them to be disregarded or lightly regarded by an all-knowing Creator. This claim implies that there is a morally important advantage in believing that if there is a God He is morally very good. I think that this practical argument for believing (K) is sound, if the theoretical argument is not.

In closing, I shall permit myself an argument *ad hominem*. The hypothesis that there is an amoral God is not open to the best known objection to theism, the argument from evil. Whatever may be said against the design argument for theism, it is at least far from obvious that the world was not designed. Yet hardly any philosopher really takes seriously the hypothesis that it was designed by an amoral or evil being. Are there any good grounds for rejecting that hypothesis? Only moral grounds. One ought to reflect on that before asserting that moral arguments are out of place in these matters.[26]

NOTES

1. Cf. Henry Sidgwick, *The Methods of Ethics*, 7th ed. (New York: Dover, 1966), p. 509: "Those who hold that the edifice of physical science is really constructed of conclusions inferred from self-evident premises, may reasonably demand that any practical judgments claiming philosophic certainty should be based on an equally firm foundation. If on the other hand we find that in our supposed knowledge of the world of nature propositions are commonly taken to be universally true, which yet seem to rest on no other grounds than that we have a strong disposition to accept them, and that they are indispensable to the systematic coherence of our beliefs,—it will be more difficult to reject a similarly supported assumption in ethics, without opening the door to universal scepticism." (Sidgwick is discussing the legitimacy of postulating, on ethical grounds, a coincidence of self-interest with duty.) Cf. also A. E. Taylor, *Does God Exist?* (London: Macmillan, 1945), p. 84f.

2. A theistic Argument from the Nature of Right and Wrong, proposed by Hastings Rashdall (*The Theory of Good and Evil* [Oxford: Clarendon Press, 1907], pp. 206-20) and taken up by W. R. Sorley (*Moral Values and the Idea of God* [Cambridge University Press, 1921], pp. 346-53) and A. E. Taylor (*Does God Exist?* p. 92f.), focuses on the question of ontological status rather than validity. It is not clear to me exactly what view those authors meant to take of the relation between God's will and moral truths.

3. Robert Merrihew Adams, "A Modified Divine Command Theory of Ethical Wrongness," in Gene Outka and John P. Reeder, Jr., eds., *Religion and Morality: A Collection of Essays* (Garden City, N.Y.: Doubleday Anchor, 1973), pp. 318-47. I take a somewhat different view here, laying more emphasis on questions of property-identity, and less on questions of meaning, than in my earlier work.

4. Here and in this discussion generally my debt to recent treatments, by Saul Kripke and others, of the relations between modality and property-identity is obvious.

5. A very similar modification is proposed by Richard B. Brandt in *Ethical Theory* (Englewood Cliffs, N.J.: Prentice-Hall, 1959), p. 73f. Brandt explicitly envisages a naturalistic version of the theory, however, thereby giving up, in my opinion, an important advantage of the divine command theory.

6. Perhaps it is necessary that if a loving God commanded killing in such circumstances, He would cause us to feel otherwise than we do about killing. But our belief is not: it is wrong for us to kill in these situations so long as we (and/or people generally) feel as we do about it. We believe rather: our feelings indicate to us a moral fact about such killing that is not a fact about our feelings.

7. Immanuel Kant, *Critique of Practical Reason*, trans. L. W. Beck (New York: Liberal Arts Press, 1956), p. 130 (p. 125 of the Prussian Academy edition).

8. C. D. Broad, in his review of A. E. Taylor's *The Faith of a Moralist* (*Mind*, 40 [1931], 364-75), neatly distills from Taylor a recognizable but interestingly different variant of Kant's theoretical argument. But that version still does not persuade me.

9. Immanuel Kant, *Religion within the Limits of Reason Alone*, trans. T. M. Greene and H. H. Hudson (New York: Harper, 1960), pp. 5-7. (The long footnote is particularly important.) In the *Critique of Practical Reason*, pp. 147-51 (142-46, Prussian Academy edition), Kant seems to me to be presenting his argument predominantly as practical, but less clearly so than in the later work. In my reading of Kant I owe much to Allen Wood, *Kant's Moral Religion* (Ithaca: Cornell University Press, 1970).

10. One thinks of Comte, Durkheim, Weber, and Parsons.

11. Here I am indebted to R. M. Hare, "The Simple Believer," in Outka and Reeder, eds., pp. 412-14. Actually Hare proposes what I would call a theoretical moral argument. He seems to think that no set of moral principles could be right unless following them would generally turn out for the best (best from a moral point of view, that is). From this and from the belief that some (intuitively acceptable) set of moral principles is right, it follows that there is such a moral order of the universe that following some (intuitively acceptable) set of moral principles will generally turn out for the best. Of course many utilitarians would say that there is such a moral order in the universe with or without God. I am not so sure as Hare that it is a theoretical requirement that following moral principles must generally turn out for the the best if the principles are correct, but his idea can at least be used in a practical argument.

12. It is not necessary to discuss here to what extent I am agreeing or disagreeing with Kant's views about the motives that a morally good person should have.

13. 1903, reprinted in Bertrand Russell, *Why I Am Not A Christian, and Other Essays on Religion and Related Subjects* (New York: Simon and Schuster, n.d.).

14. William James, "The Sentiment of Rationality," in his *The Will to Believe and Other Essays in Popular Philosophy* (New York: Dover Publications, 1956), p. 97.

15. William James, "The Will to Believe," ibid., p. 1I. The terminology of "living," "forced," and "momentous options" comes from the same essay.

16. This paragraph was inspired by a similar remark on the variety of intellectual virtues by Nicholas Wolterstorff.

17. Cf. David Hume, *An Enquiry Concerning Human Understanding*, Section X, Part I, 4th paragraph.

18. Sigmund Freud, *The Future of an Illusion*, trans. by W. D. Robson-Scott, rev. by James Strachey (Garden City, N.Y.: Doubleday Anchor, 1964). Freud thought (though he expressed uncertainty) that society could learn to get along without this function of religion. A vivid ancient Greek statement of this reason for prizing belief in gods is quoted by Wallace I. Matson, *The Existence of God* (Ithaca: Cornell University Press, 1965), p. 221f.

19. See Michael Argyle, *Religious Behaviour* (London: Routledge & Kegan Paul, 1958), pp. 96–99.

20. Cf. John Stuart Mill, *Utility of Religion*, ed., with Mill's *Nature*, by George Nakhnikian (New York: Liberal Arts Press, 1958), p. 62: "The value of religion as a supplement to human laws, a more cunning sort of police, an auxiliary to the thief-catcher and the hangman, is not that part of its claims which the more high-minded of its votaries are fondest of insisting on; and they would probably be as ready as anyone to admit that, if the nobler offices of religion in the soul could be dispensed with, a substitute might be found for so coarse and selfish a social instrument as the fear of hell. In their view of the matter, the best of mankind absolutely require religion for the perfection of their own character, even though the coercion of the worst might possibly be accomplished without its aid."

21. Cf. the interesting argument on the relevance of faith in a moral order of the universe to child-rearing in Peter L. Berger, *A Rumor of Angels* (Garden City, N.Y.: Doubleday, 1969), pp. 66–71.

22. The attempt to discover or prove such a harmony has been one of the recurrent preoccupations of moral theory. Sidgwick thought it might be necessary to postulate "a connexion of Virtue and self-interest" in order to avoid "an ultimate and fundamental contradiction in our apparent intuitions of what is Reasonable in conduct" (*The Methods of Ethics*, p. 508). This led him into what may fairly be described as a flirtation with a moral argument for faith in a moral world-order if not in God. He believed that our intuitions endorse both the principle that one ought always to do what will maximize one's own happiness and the principle that one ought always to do what will maximize the happiness of all. But these principles cannot both be true unless there is a moral order of the universe by virtue of which the act that maximizes universal happiness always maximizes the agent's happiness too. I think Sidgwick's reasoning claims too much obligatoriness for the egoistic principle. But the inspiration for the argument I present in the text came originally from him and from William K. Frankena, "Sidgwick and the Dualism of Practical Reason," *The Monist*, 58 (1974), 449–67.

23. I take Philippa Foot to be suggesting this in "Morality as a System of Hypothetical Imperatives," *The Philosophical Review*, 81 (1972), 305–16.

24. *The Methods of Ethics*, p. 507n.

25. A theistic argument from the nature of guilt has been offered by A. E. Taylor, *The Faith of a Moralist*, vol. I (London: Macmillan, 1930), pp. 206-10. Cf. also H. P. Owen, *The Moral Argument for Christian Theism* (London: George Allen & Unwin, 1965), pp. 57-59.

26. I have discussed the topics of this paper for several years in classes at the University of Michigan and UCLA, with students and colleagues to whom I am indebted in more ways than I can now remember. I am particularly grateful to Thomas E. Hill, Jr., Bernard Kobes, and Barry Miller for their comments on the penultimate draft.

What Is It to Believe Someone?

G. E. M. ANSCOMBE

There were three men, A, B and C, talking in a certain village. A said "If that tree falls down, it'll block the road for a long time." "That's not so if there's a tree-clearing machine working," said B. C remarked "There *will* be one, if the tree doesn't fall down." The famous sophist Euthydemus, a stranger in the place, was listening. He immediately said "I believe you all. So I infer that the tree will fall and the road will be blocked."

Question: What's wrong with Euthydemus?

Believing someone is not merely a neglected topic in philosophical discussion; it seems to be unknown. I have found people experiencing difficulty in grasping it from the title —found them assuming, for example, that I must really mean "believing *in* someone." How do I mean, believing someone? If you told me you had eaten sausages for breakfast, I would believe you. The thing itself is extremely familiar. Does it deserve the attention of a philosophic enquirer? I hope to show that it does. It is of great importance in philosophy and in life, and it is itself problematic enough to need philosophical investigation.

If words always kept their old values, I might have called my subject "Faith." That short term has in the past been used in just this meaning, of believing someone. (Of course that term had also other meanings like *loyalty*, etc.) This old meaning has a vestige in such an expression as "You merely took it on faith"—i.e., you believed someone without further enquiry or consideration. This is only actually *said* as a reproach—but it is often true when it is not blameworthy.

At one time, there was the following way of speaking: faith was distinguished as human and divine. Human faith was believing a mere human being; divine faith was believing God. Occurring in discussion without any qualifying adjective, the word "faith" tended to mean only or mostly 'divine faith'. But its value in this line of descent has quite altered. Nowadays it is used to mean much the same thing as 'religion' or possibly 'religious belief'. Thus belief in God would now generally be called 'faith'—belief in God at all, not belief that God will help one, for example. This is a great pity. It has had a disgusting effect on thought about religion. The astounding idea that there should be such a thing as *believing God* has been lost sight of. "Abraham believed God, and that counted as his justification." Hence he was called "the father of faith." Even in this rather well-known context where the words appear plainly, they are not attended to. The story itself has indeed remained well known even to ignorant intellectuals mainly because of the thoughts of the fictitious author Johannes de Silentio.* Interesting as these thoughts are, we should notice that the author gets into the territory of his interest by cunningly evading the first point of the story, that *Abraham believed God.* He knows it is there, but he does not confront it. This has had its effect; for in matters of intellectual fashion we tend to be like sheep. And so, even though the words appear plainly, they are not, it seems, reflected on. Rather, we are deluged with rubbish about 'believing in' as opposed to 'believing that'. Like the chorus of animals in Orwell, there is a *claque* chanting "believing in goo-ood, believing that ba-ad."

Naturally anyone thinking on those lines won't take an interest in belief with a personal object. For that is necessarily always also 'believing that'. It is indeed convenient, and for my purposes all but necessary, to coin the form of expression: believing *x* that *p*.

Fear and Trembling, to be obtained from booksellers by citing the author S. Kierkegaard.

I am not interested here in any sense of 'believing in ————'
except that in which it means 'believing that ——— exists'.
This belief, with God as argument, could not be "divine
faith." This comes out quite clearly if we use my suggested
form: believing x that p. It would be bizarre to say that one
believed N that N existed. Let us consider the most favorable
case for this being possible: an unheard-of relation, who writes
to you out of the blue to apprise you of his existence and
circumstances. Believing that he does indeed exist is accepting
the letter as genuinely what it purports to be, and hence that
the writer is who he says he is. If you do accept that, you may
believe more things—as, that he has a sheep farm in New
South Wales—on his say-so. That will be believing him. But
the actual existence of the ostensible *he*, whose say-so this
is, cannot be believed in the same manner. "He says he exists,
and I suppose he knows and doesn't mean to deceive me."

My topic is important not only for theology and for the
philosophy of religion. It is also of huge importance for the
theory of knowledge. The greater part of our knowledge of
reality rests upon the belief that we repose in things we have
been taught and told. Hume thought that the idea of cause-
and-effect was the bridge enabling us to reach any idea of a
world beyond personal experience. He wanted to subsume
belief in testimony under belief in causes and effects, or at
least to class them together as examples of the same form of
belief. We believe in a cause, he thought, because we perceive
the effect and cause and effect have been found always to go
together. Similarly we believe in the truth of testimony because
we perceive the testimony and we have (well! often have) found
testimony and truth to go together! The view needs only to
be stated to be promptly rejected. It was always absurd, and
the mystery is how Hume could ever have entertained it. We
must acknowledge testimony as giving us our larger world
in no smaller degree, or even in a greater degree, than the
relation of cause and effect; and believing it is quite dissimilar
in structure from belief in causes and effects. Nor is what testimony gives us entirely a detachable part, like the thick fringe
of fat on a chunk of steak. It is more like the flecks and streaks

of fat that are often distributed through good meat; though there are lumps of pure fat as well. Examples could be multiplied indefinitely. You have received letters; how did you ever learn what a letter was and how it came to you? You will take up a book and look in a certain place and see "New York, Dodd Mead and Company, 1910." So do you know from personal observation that that book was published by that company, and then, and in New York? Well, hardly. But you do know it *purports* to have been so. How? Well, you know that is where the publisher's name is always put, and the name of the place where his office belongs. How do you know that? You were taught it. What you were taught was your tool in acquiring the new knowledge. "There was an American edition" you will say, "I've seen it." Think how much reliance on believing what you have been told lies behind being able to say that. It is irrelevant at this level to raise a question about possible forgery; without what we know by testimony, there is no such thing as what a forgery is *pretending* to be.

You may think you know that New York is in North America. What is New York, what is North America? You may say you have been in these places. But how much does that fact contribute to your knowledge? Nothing, in comparison with testimony. How did you know you were there? Even if you inhabit New York and you have simply learned its name as the name of the place you inhabit, there is the question: How extensive a region is this place you are calling "New York"? And what has New York got to do with this bit of a map? Here is a complicated network of received information.

With this as preamble, let us begin an investigation.

'Believe' with personal object cannot be reflexive. Since one can tell oneself things, that may seem odd. We shall see why it is so later.

One might think at first blush that to believe another is simply to believe what he says, or believe that what he says is true. But that is not so, for one may already believe the thing he says. (If you tell me "Napoleon lost the battle of

Waterloo" and I say "I believe you," that is a joke.) Again, what someone's saying a thing may bring about, is that one forms one's *own* judgment that the thing is true. In teaching philosophy we do not hope that our pupils will *believe us,* but rather, that they will *come to see* that what we say is true —if it is.

A witness might be asked "Why did you think the man was dying?" and reply "Because the doctor told me." If asked further what his own judgment was, he may reply "I had no opinion of my own—I just believed the doctor." This brings out how believing *x* that *p* involves relying on *x* for it that *p*. And so one might think that believing someone is believing something on the strength of his saying that it is so. But even that is not right. For suppose I were convinced that B wished to deceive me, and would tell the opposite of what he believed, but that on the matter in hand B would be believing the opposite of the truth. By calculation on this, then, I believe what B says, on the strength of his saying it—but only in a comical sense can I be said to believe *him.**

Now we have the solution to the puzzle which I set at the head of this essay. Euthydemus' utterance is crazy. But why? If logic is concerned only with what follows from what, his logic is impeccable. The conjunction of A's and B's remarks implies that there will be no machine working; from that and C's contribution we derive that the tree will fall. Why then is Euthydemus' remark so off-key? The answer is, that he cannot be telling the truth when he says "I believe you all." He cannot be believing A at that stage of *that* conversation, unless A still purports to believe what he said. But A does not purport so to believe if he gives no sign, and if what B said is not merely true, but also as pertinent as it must be if what C said is true. The assumption that A privately sticks to what he said, indeed, makes it questionable what he meant, i.e., what thought lay behind A's saying "If the tree falls, the road will be blocked." (It might for example be the conviction that the tree *will* fall and block the road.) Now Euthydemus makes

---

*This case was described to me in discussion by Mary Geach.

no check on A; he does not wait a moment to see how A reacts
to what B and C say. The natural way to understand B's
remark is to take it as casting doubt on what A said, and that
is what makes Euthydemus' "I believe you all" so insane.
For *insane* is just what Euthydemus' remark is and sounds—
it is not, for example, like the expression of a somewhat
rash opinion, or of excessive credulity.

We also see why one cannot "believe oneself" when one
tells oneself something. To believe N one must believe that N
himself believes what he is saying.

So far we have considered cases of believing people who are
perceived. But often all we have is the communication without
the speaker. This is so almost any time we find something out
because it is told us in a book.

Of course we may be handed the book by a teacher who tells
us something about the author. Then we have a communication
with a perceived person communicating; and this is about
another communication where the communicator is unper-
ceived. It is interesting that when we are introduced to books
as sources of information in our childhood it does not usually
go like that. We are taught to consult books like oracles, and
the idea of the author is not much brought to our attention at
first. In any case, after a time we come to receive communications in books without anyone introducing them to us, and we
are apt to believe—as we put it—what the book says about
itself; for example that it was printed by a certain printer.

To believe a person is not necessarily to treat him as an
original authority. He is *an* original authority on what he
himself has done and seen and heard: I say *an* original authority because I only mean that he does himself contribute something, e.g., is in some sort a witness, as opposed to one who only
transmits information received. But his account of what he is a
witness to is very often, as in the example of there being an
American edition, heavily affected or rather all but completely
formed by what information *he* had received. I do not mean
that if he says "I ate an apple this morning" he is relying on
information that that was an apple; if he is in the situation
usual among us, he knows what an apple is—i.e., can recognize
one. So, though he was "taught the concept" in learning to use

language in everyday life, I do not count that as a case of reliance on information received. But if he says he saw a picture by Leonardo da Vinci, that *is* such a case. He has necessarily depended on some tradition of information. Thus a speaker may be a total original authority for the fact that he gives, as would usually be the case if one of us said he had eaten an apple, or *an* original authority, but not a total one, as if he says he saw some of Leonardo's drawings; or he may not be an original authority at all, as if he says that Leonardo made drawings for a flying machine. In this latter case he almost certainly knows it from having been told, *even* if he's seen the drawings. (It is true that he *might* have "discovered it for himself." If so, then all the same he has relied on information received that these are Leonardo drawings; or that drawings like to these are Leonardo drawings; and he has noticed—*here* he is an original authority —that *these* drawings are drawings of a flying machine; that *Leonardo* made drawings for flying machines will then be inference on his part.)

When he knows it just from being told (as most of us do) then, as I say, he is in no way an original authority. But that does not mean that there is no such thing as believing *him*. Much information is acquired from teachers who are not original authorities, and their pupils who acquire it believe *them*. As opposed to what? As opposed to merely believing that what they say is true. Consider belief reposed in what an interpreter says—I mean the case of believing the sentences he comes out with. If you believe those communications, probably—i.e., in the normal case—you are believing his principal: your reliance on the interpreter is only belief that he has reproduced what his principal said. But *he* is not wrong if what he says is untrue, so long as it does not falsely represent what his principal said. A teacher, on the other hand, even though in no way an original authority, *is* wrong if what he says is untrue, and that hangs together with the fact that his pupils believe (or disbelieve) *him*.

These various considerations draw attention to the further beliefs that are involved in believing someone. First of all, it must be the case that you believe that something is a communication from him (or "from someone") and second, you have to believe that by it he means to be telling you *this*. It is important

for us that natural noises and visual phenomena do not usually
sound or look like language, that the question whether someone
is speaking or whether this is a bit of written language is hardly
ever a difficult one to answer. Someone who saw the markings
of leaves as language and strove to decipher them as messages,
possibly directed to himself, would strike us as demented. And
this brings out another aspect: that the communication is
addressed to someone, even if only to "whom it may concern,"
or "the passer-by" or "whoever may happen in the future to
read this."

We see, then, that various questions arise: (1) Suppose that
someone gets hold of written communications, but they are not
addressed to him at all, not even meant to reach him. Can he
be said to believe the writer if he believes what they tell the
addressee? Only in a reduced or extended sense, though the
matter is perhaps not of any importance. (2) Suppose someone
gets a written communication which is addressed to him, but
the actual writer—I mean the author—is not the ostensible communicator. For example, I write letters to someone as from a
pen-friend in Oklahoma. Can the recipient be said to believe
(or disbelieve) either the actual author or the ostensible communicator? Surely not the former, except in a very special case
and in a roundabout way: I mean, he might himself discern
that this comes from the actual writer, myself; and judge that
I was trying to tell him something. But otherwise not. This
case, where there is intervening judgment and speculation,
should alert us to the fact that in the most ordinary cases of
believing someone, there is no such mediation. In order to
believe NN, one "must believe" that, e.g., this is a communication from NN; but that is not believing in the sense of forming
a judgment. If one learned it was not a communication from
NN, one would straightway cease to say one was believing NN.
Now can the recipient, if he *is* deceived, be said to believe or
disbelieve the ostensible communicator? Here we have to consider two distinct cases, according as the ostensible communicator exists or not. If he does not exist, then the decision to speak
of 'believing him' or 'disbelieving him' is a decision to give
those verbs an "intentional" use, like the verb 'to look for'. "The
child had an imaginary companion whom he called Efelin and

who told him all sorts of things—he always believed Efelin."
And so one might speak of someone as believing the god
(Apollo, say), when he consulted the oracle of the god—without
thereby implying that one believed in the existence of that god
oneself. All we want is that we should know what is called the
god's telling him something.

If on the other hand the ostensible communicator does
exist, then a third party may be the less likely to use the verb
'believe' "intentionally," i.e., to say "So, thinking that NN
said this, he believed him." But it is an intelligible way of
speaking. And NN himself might say "I see, you thought I said
this, and you believed me." If the recipient, however, says
"Naturally I believed *you*," NN might reject this, saying "Since
I didn't say it, you weren't believing me." Thus there is an
oscillation here in the use of the notion of believing and disbelieving a person.

(3) This comes out in another way where the recipient does
not believe that the communication *is* from NN. This, it seems,
lets him off the hook of any reproach from NN about his not
having believed him, not having done what he asked, and so on.
But may not NN have a complaint at the very doubt whether
a communication that *is* from him, really is so? It depends on
the circumstances; but NN may well regard it as an evasion, if
the recipient seizes on the possibility of treating the communication as not coming from him when it did. NN may call it a
refusal to believe him.

(4) If X is to believe NN, something must be being taken as
a communication, and since X must be believing something
"on NN's say-so," there is also involved the belief that *this*
communication says such-and-such. This may seem absurd;
surely I may simply believe *your words*, and not have a different
version of their meaning and say that what you said meant *that*.
On the other hand I ought to be able to elaborate upon anything
that I believe: to be able to say who is being referred to, or what
time, or what sort of action if I am told, and believe, e.g., "John's
daughter eloped at Christmas." Nor are one's beliefs tied to
particular words; one reproduces the gist of what one has been
told in various ways, and so there is, after all, room for the
belief that *that* communication told one such-and-such. So when

someone says that he believes such-and-such because he believes NN, we may say "We suspect a misunderstanding. What did you take as NN's telling you that?"

Now, therefore, instead of speaking of the "actual writer"—by whom in the case of the pen-friend I understood the author—we can speak of the immediate producer of what is taken, or makes an internal claim to be taken, as a communication from NN. Such a producer may be a messenger, anyone who "passes on" some communication, or an interpreter (translator) of it. And the recipient can at any rate *fail to believe* (as opposed to disbelieving) NN out of a variety of attitudes. He may not notice the communication at all. He may notice it but not take it as language. He may notice it and take it as language but not make anything of it. He may notice it and take it as language and make something of it but not take it as addressed to himself. Or he may notice it and take it as language and yet, whether or not he takes it as addressed to himself, he may make the wrong thing of it. And he may take it as addressed to himself and not make the wrong thing of it but not believe that it comes from NN.

Only when we have excluded all the cases—or, more probably, simply *assumed* their exclusion—do we come to the situation in which the question simply is: Does X believe NN or not? That is to say, there are many presuppositions to that question as we ordinarily understand it.

It is an insult and it may be an injury not to be believed. At least it is an insult if one is oneself made aware of the refusal, and it may be an injury if others are. Note that here the difference between disbelief and suspension of judgment is of less importance than where the object is only a proposition and not a person. And failure of some of the presuppositions allows scope for reproach. If A has not believed that something was a message from NN when it was, or has given it some false interpretation, NN may (perhaps justly) see in this a readiness on A's part not to believe him. And even if A has falsely believed that something *was* a message from NN and has disbelieved it, while NN cannot say (except in an extended sense) "You disbelieved me!" he may be able to say "You showed yourself very ready to disbelieve me." Or: "You showed yourself ready to credit me with saying something that could not be worthy of belief." For it would be a megalomaniac who complained of not being believed, when he agrees that the thing that was not believed was, anyway, not true. Falsehood lets one off all hooks. Compare the irritation of a teacher at not being believed. On the whole, such irritation is just—in matters where learners must learn by believing teachers. But if what was not believed should turn out to be false, his complaint collapses.

Let us suppose that all the presuppositions are in. A is then in the situation—a very normal one—where the question arises of believing or doubting (suspending judgment in face of) NN. Unconfused by all the questions that arise because of the presuppositions, we can see that believing someone (in the particular case) is trusting him for the truth—in the particular case.

I will end with a problem. I imagined the case where I believed what someone told me, and got the information from his telling me, but did not believe *him*. This was because I believed he would tell me what he thought was false, but also would be clean wrong in what he thought. Now I *may*—it is not the normal case, but it certainly occurs—have to reflect on whether someone is likely to be right and truthful in a particular case when he is telling me that *p*. If I conclude that he is, I will then believe him that *p*. I think it is clear that this could not be the case for learners, at least elementary learners or young children. But someone might say: "What is the difference between the two cases, culminating in belief that *p* because NN has told one that *p*? In both cases there is calculation; in one, you believe what the man says as a result of a calculation that he is a liar but wrong, and in the other, you calculate that he is truthful and right. (No belief in his *general* truthfulness is involved.) The difference between the two cases is only as stated. When you say that in the first case you do not believe *the man*, only what he tells you, and in the second you believe the man, that is just a bit of terminology: you are only willing to *call* it believing the man when you believe he is right and truthful in intent.

It appears to me that there is more to be said than that about the priority of rightness and truthfulness in this matter, but I am not clear what it is.

Religion and Faith in
St. Augustine's *Confessions*

FREDERICK CROSSON

The intent of this essay is first, to delineate three ways in which human beings have tried to gain a perspective on and make sense of the whole within we live, and second, to argue that not only are these ways successively exemplified in St. Augustine's story of his first thirty-three years, but that they serve to disclose a specific meaning and structure in his *Confessions*. So, the general movement is from conceptual analysis to instantiation in a historical text, involving the employment of the concepts in the interpretation of the text.

The three ways are characterized first of all by their respective typical modes of discourse. We encounter these modes as different kinds of texts, but it is not irrelevant to note in each case an oral tradition precedes and conditions the textual tradition in important ways. St. Paul's statement that faith comes through hearing not only reflects the fact that oral kerygma was the primary means of communicating in the first century, but it attests to the power of the spoken word, which can bear witness in a way impossible for a written text. St. Augustine's astonishment, recorded in the sixth book of the *Confessions*, that anyone would read a text silently also manifests the distance which sets our print culture apart from his, and of which we might otherwise be unaware.[1]

Herodotus already distinguishes *mythos*, *logos*, and *istoria* as three kinds of discourse: we might translate them as fabulation, giving an account of something, and inquiry which takes the form of narration, respectively. 'Philosophy' here will be taken to refer to the kind of reasoned account which Plato and Aristotle brought to maturity; the Bible will be taken to be historical at least in Herodotus' sense, as embodying the results of inquiry into the meaning of certain past events.

I

Myths and sacred histories may share a narrative mode, but the difference between them is not that the one is fabricated while the other is anchored in real past events. For, on the one hand, man does not make up myths out of whole cloth. Similar archetypal images, events, and structures occur in myths all over the world. At the core of these mythical stories are images which press themselves upon a people's conscious imagination and whose congruity with some deeper strata of the soul is reflected in their cultural potency.

On the other hand, it is not simply the anchorage in real events which specifies that mode of history which serves as the adequate embodiment of a people's fundamental beliefs: what characterizes it is that the events are perceived as the actions— direct or indirect—of God. Indeed, the empirical reality of the events is often so suffused by their spiritual meaning that memory retains the former only dimly. Here it is not the universal images which dominate the narration, but the reporting of God's action and of the coming of His word.

Philosophy's situation in this configuration is complex: as the critical reflection of reason on the presuppositions and implications of what is given, its relation to the other two forms of articulating fundamental beliefs varies according to what is received as given. Reason may stand with the belief modes, in the service of their clarification, e.g., in the forms of systematic theology or of commentary on a sacred text. Or, reason may discern an independent ground of evidence for its judgments and adopt a critical or complementary attitude toward the sacred text. Or finally, reason may bracket or ignore the sacred texts and proceed to elaborate its own view of the whole.

Whether the last attempt can respond to reason's heart is an open question. Even if philosophical reason infers the existence of the divine, an inferred God is an absent God. *Dieu sensible au coeur,* God present to one's heart, was the way Pascal characterized faith. What would seem to mark both religion in general and faith in particular is a sense—not merely an intellectual conviction—of the presence of the divine. That sense of presence ranges from the vivid experience of the mystic or of the sudden convert to the more diffuse awareness acknowledged in ritual prayers, communal or personal, from group silences (Quakers) to dances and liturgical meals.

The stance adopted here is that of a philosophical reflection on religion and faith, a reflection which stands on independent grounds in the sense of appealing to its own evidence but which, in forming its own view of the whole, seeks to understand the ground and evidence of religion and faith as embodying a sense of the whole. Religion and faith typically ignore, if they do not spurn, the appeal to purely rational grounds of evidence. They do not seek to persuade by such appeals, but rather simply to hand on that understanding whose acceptance has constituted them. Intelligent reflection can indeed play an important part in the development of what is handed on, but its appeals are to the sacred stories themselves and to the world precisely as structured in its meaning by the stories. Apologetics is not intrinsic to that development. (So Augustine writes his *Confessions* for his fellow-believers: X, 3 and 4).

Moreover, religion bases itself on recourse to long-elapsed epochs, to an earlier cycle of things, or to a qualitatively different beginning time (the age of Kronos, as Plato says) in telling how things came to be the way they are. But philosophy by its very nature must appeal to what is accessible *semper et ubique* to reason, to what can be seen, guided by the philosopher's words. Faith, just because historical events are the primary locus of the disclosure of God, bridges this division which sets religion and philosophy over against each other; while recounting the past wonderful acts of God, it looks toward His manifesting of Himself at any time.

To explore these relations further, let us turn to one of the greatest of those who philosophized in faith, Thomas Aquinas.

He distinguishes religion and faith in a number of ways, the most fundamental of which is by defining religion as a natural moral virtue and faith as a supernatural virtue whose seat is the intellect. Moral virtues take doings as their object, *agibilia*, things-to-be-done. (Faith, in contrast, has truth as its object, specifically the First Truth, God.)

Two consequences follow from this categorization of religion. First, religion is not focused on experiences (I am not sure Aquinas would make any sense out of "religious experience") but on certain kinds of actions, and second, religion designates a social mode of behavior, because it deals with the relation which human beings have with a superior being.

Aquinas considers religion to be a part of justice: the virtue which orients appropriately man's relations with God. He accepts Cicero's definition of religion as "the offering of service and ceremonial rites to a superior nature that men call divine." Recall that Thomas, following Aristotle, conceives moral virtues to be dispositions to which man is naturally adapted or inclined. Nevertheless, as Aristotle put it, "none of the moral virtues arises in us by nature." We have to create the forms of moral behavior, fitting them progressively to our progressively determined disposition.

Just as life in a political community is natural in their view, yet each polis must be constructed by human intelligence and energy, dimly and diversely guided by a sense of what is just and good, so the developing virtue of religion creates highly diversified forms of ritual and story, attempting to understand and respond to the *chiaroscuro* of a sensed presence of the divine, a presence felt to be naturally ambient in the inhabited cosmos. What is striking in the rich proliferation of symbolic images and actions in the world's religions is the existence of an apparently converging set of patterns in the myths and rituals which exhibit what may be called a natural expression of the religious response.

However that may be, the appropriate understanding of the divine nature is corrected and clarified in the teaching of the acknowledged masters in the "higher religions," where the cognitive inadequacy of the spontaneous symbols is perceived. But two observations are pertinent here: one is that the religious

instinct of the common worshipper continues to generate and
cling to the symbols as vehicles not only of understanding, but
of communion with and of protection against the numinous
character of the objects of worship. The second observation is
that that instinct of the common worshipper is not unwise; the
way of symbols, the way of affirmations is as important as the
way of negation of symbols (i.e. the perception of their inadequacy) in the quest for understanding.

Faith—I characterize it here descriptively, not theologically
—arises within a religious matrix and continues to coexist with
the phenomena of the religious function. Like religion and
unlike philosophy, it corresponds to an affirmed presence of
the divine, but is distinguished by a characteristic form of
expression, the recounting of the historical narratives. As noted
above, however, this is a generic description. What specifies
sacred history is the vision of a second level of unique meaning
in the historical events: the actions of a God who deals with His
people in and through the things which befall them. Religion,
too, finds distinctive meaning in the situations of life, but it
is by the assimilation of those situations to timeless paradigms,
to the typical models of gods and goddesses and their stories:
the cycle of Karma, or of the Buddhist Kalpa, the re-enactment
of the creation story at the beginning of the New Year, the
re-incarnating of the perfect marriage of Shiva and Parvati or
of Rama and Sita. Faith, insofar as it inevitably coexists with
the religious functions shares some of this paradigmatic
understanding—e.g., Christianity re-enacting the creation
story at the liturgy of the vernal equinox, or modeling marriage
on the family of Nazareth. But it adds an essentially novel and
individual dimension by understanding the possibility that
that second level of meaning may be uniquely addressed to me,
peculiar to the events of my life.

There is, clearly, a tension between religion and faith despite
their similarities vis-à-vis philosophy. "Demythologization"
and "religionless Christianity" are contemporary expressions
of that tension, attempts to purge away the dross of religious
overgrowth. But the constant accretion of superstition and
of magic onto Christianity in many countries (including our
own) suggests that faith does not normally perdure except in

symbiotic relations with religious symbols which are not peculiar to it. Indeed, the scriptural history in which faith narrates the objects of its belief makes use of the same common religious symbols in specific historical instantiations; think of the book of Exodus or the Gospel of John.

Philosophy of religion cannot ignore these symbols, because it is through their meaning that the divine first comes into human apprehension. But it is not limited to them in attempting critically to understand the religious function and to ground the existence and nature of the divinity which the symbols intend. Founded on its own evidence, philosophy of religion is a complementary discipline, part natural theology, part reflection on the phenomena of religion and faith. With respect to the latter phenomena, the philosopher is situated in a manner similar to his reflection on political life; he must seek first to understand those human attitudes in the terms in which they present themselves to the believer rather than from the outside. I do not mean that he must be a believer, but that just as the political philosopher begins from the terms in which political life is lived—discussions about what is good or just or right and wrong for the community—and seeks to clarify and deepen our understanding of those categories (rather than approach politics as a power game of who gets what, when and how), so the philosopher of religion must begin from the specific character of what people say and do when they are relating themselves to what is holy. In the one as in the other case, the formulation of questions about the reality of justice or of God must be guided by the understanding which the ordinary language of the citizen and the believer embodies.

We shall see that Augustine passes successively through each of these modes of making sense of the whole. His religious beliefs succumb to a philosophic and scientific critique, to be replaced in turn by a conversion to faith, to Catholic Christianity.

II

When he was nineteen years old, already conducting a school at Thagaste, Augustine came across Cicero's *Hortensius*, an exhortation to follow the philosophic life. Reading it was a profoundly moving experience for him. It awakened an awareness of the possibility and desirability of wisdom, of a view of the whole by which to orient one's life. He turned to the Scriptures, which had been until then the half-conscious but unassessed basis of his life. In comparison with Cicero, they appeared unworthy to provide such a vision, and before the year was out, he became an auditor in the Manichean sect, which presented itself to him as an intellectually and emotionally satisfying religious wisdom.

"Fantasies and phantoms" he was later to call these teachings, but for a long time this gnostic dualism of good and evil, of light and darkness, of spirit and flesh provided at least a tentative view of the whole by which he understood and guided his life.

Still, one of the wonderful things about St. Augustine was that, for all his religious passion, he never "lost his head." Prosyletizing and practicing Manichean that he was for nine years, he rejected that religion when it became apparent that it was irreconcilable with what he *knew* about astronomy, about solstices and eclipses and the motions of the planets.[2] And when he became a Christian, he never ceased to question the meaning of the tradition he received and to confirm its truth by the touchstone of his own understanding and experience.

He did not think that everyone needed to do this; indeed he thought that some were better off not bothering their heads about it. But for him, the desire for understanding was not assuaged by faith. On the contrary, it seems to have been increased by his conversion.

The turn away from Manicheanism, initiated by his encounter with Faustus in Carthage, was followed by a period of intellectual drifting, a seeking of moorings without success. He was attracted at first by the skepticism of the Academics, a not unusual attraction in those who come to see that what they held for certain was not certain (V,10; VI,4).

But Augustine was, on reflection, convinced that there was a large class of everyday ordinary beliefs which, if their certainty was not demonstrated or even demonstrable, could hardly be doubted on rational grounds. Beliefs about events in the past, about other places, about those he conversed with fell into this category (VI,4).

The doctrinal philosophers, especially Epicurus, now became more plausible to him, but materialism seemed unacceptable on moral grounds (VI,16). And so finally he encountered what afterwards appeared to him the antechamber of Christianity, "certain books of the Platonists." The teaching of these books was the closest Augustine came to a satisfying view of the whole based on reason. Ultimately philosophy remained for him what it had been for Plato, the love of wisdom rather than the possession of it.

Hence, it is not strange that when he turned to Christianity, he understood it as the fulfillment of the wisdom sought by the philosophers. In the little dialogue *On the Teacher (De Magistro)* written just after his conversion, for example, although he identifies Christ with the light by which the soul knows, the explication of *what* the soul knows is wholly addressed to natural signs, to natural knowledge. It is through Christ as the light that the upper part of the Divided Line becomes accessible. Yet when he returns to the subject of language in the *Confessions*, it is no longer the question of natural signs which holds the foreground, but rather the question of how it is that historical events can become signs.

Consider the problem of language in the *Confessions*. In his view, language learning rests originally on a natural "language" of gestures, changes of countenance, nods, movements of the eyes, etc., which discriminate the actions of seeking, possessing, rejecting, avoiding, and, generally, the taking up of attitudes toward things. Words are mapped into this half-discerned landscape of actions and things by the slow apprehension of their use in various contexts, by seeing how they are "set in their proper places in different sentences".[3]

The things picked out by words referring to sensible objects and actions are retained in my memory, and I can understand discourse about such things in their absence because I can recall what they signify. Language about numbers and dimensions, on the other hand, about what literature or grammar or logic *is* (given that such language is not about any present or past sensible objects), Augustine says we recognize and understand by turning to more remote recesses of memory, to strata which open out toward undiscerned regions of the soul's world.

It is in following the unmarked path up through these regions that (in the seventh book) Augustine first apprehends God as the light which illuminates the unchanging objects of these remote regions, of this realm of eternal truths. To understand the truth of an asserted mathematical proposition, for example, is to *recognize* through the sounds a timelessly available object of our memory. Learning, understanding, is recognizing by remembering.[4]

Whatever may be said of this view, it is not formulated *ad hoc* for religious purposes. On the contrary, Augustine holds it on philosophical grounds *although* it creates a problem for the language of faith. God as the light by which eternal truths are disclosed is one thing—a historical God, the Word made flesh, is something else again. For how can we recognize *that* God, whose appearance in time is not an eternal truth? "How should I find you if I do not remember you?" he asks. "How can I recognize the reality unless I remember it?"[5]

Even apart from the weight of the Platonic tradition, it is easy to see why Augustine turned to the image of light to expound his theory of knowledge. For he found in the Gospels the confirmation of this imagery in the description of Christ as the light which enlightens every man, and it is this description which in *On the Teacher* he placed at the heart of his theory of signs.[6] But the *Confessions* is more circumspect, more sensitive to the problematical relation of truth and time than *On the Teacher*. It may be viewed as a reprise of the former dialogue, extending the notion of a sign. Memory remains the key, but it is no longer simply a Platonic doctrine of recollection.

We have talked about the periods of Augustine's life as exhibiting the sequence of religion, philosophy, and faith. In respect to the last of these, we have noted that in one way it seems a fulfillment of the philosophic quest, yet in another way it presents claims which appear to go beyond the philosophic grounds of knowability (recollection). What I want to argue now is not only that Augustine's understanding of faith both enlarged the problematic of *On the Teacher* and provided a solution to the larger problematic, but that that understanding structures the way in which he tells his confession. Not only is there a sequence of religion, philosophy, and faith, but the specific perspective of the latter provides a formal unity for the whole.

In order to approach the hermeneutics of the *Confessions*, we must look first at its structure. It has long been held that the work has no unifying formal structure. The books certainly do not represent equal portions of time, and the story seems to go in fits and starts, to digress and return. Augustine himself comments twice that he omits many things because he is hastening on to tell his confession.[7] Dominant themes can certainly be identified, but formal structure is more difficult to see. I believe that there is such a structure, but I shall not do more here than sketch enough of it for our purposes.

Augustine himself in the *Retractions* gives a first, if obvious, division of the books: "ten are about me and three are about sacred scripture."[8] And clearly, Book Ten stands apart from the others. It speaks not only from another time, but speaks almost in abstraction from time. No contemporaries are named in it, no contemporary events are discussed. The nine autobiographical books divide neatly in the middle of the middle book. There Augustine reaches the nadir of his itinerary in the encounter with Faustus, and departs for Italy, thus separating the two halves into an African and an Italian sojourn. The nine books begin with a birth and end with a death, that of Monica, of whom he says, "out of her life and mine one life had been made."[9]

If we take the central book, Five, as a breaking point and align the other books, we find correlations running serially between the two groups (1-4 and 6-9). For example, the end of Eight refers back explicitly to the end of Three, to the prophetic words of the bishop to Monica about Augustine's ultimate conversion, and Cicero's name appears only in these two, linking the two 'conversions'. Similarly Book Four dwells at length on the death of his boyhood friend, while Nine is replete with reference to the deaths of not only Monica but of Verecundus, Nebridius, and Adeodatus (with a striking contrast in Augustine's attitude toward the death of loved ones in the two books). His teaching begins in Four and ends in Nine, and his authorship occurs only in these two. And so on.

What is the meaning that is disclosed to the meditating Augustine and embodied in this structure?

In remembering the events of his life prior to his conversion, Augustine is led to see that God was present with him throughout those years, even though Augusting was oblivious to His presence and indeed felt estranged and abandoned. The early books of the *Confessions*—up to the center of Book Five—are full of verbs describing his movement down and away and falling and outward. The second half, up to the conversion in Book Eight, introduces verbs of turning and returning and rising, and, importantly, moving inward. The turn-about comes precisely in the center of the fifth book. God, with Faustus the Manichean as His unknowing instrument, frees Augustine from the "snare" of Manicheanism, and guides him, under the guise of a civil appointment first in Rome, then in Milan, toward the tutelage of St. Ambrose, Bishop of Milan.

Recall the problematic of *On the Teacher*: How is it possible that the omnipresent God is *now recognized* as having been providentially present to Augustine in those years when Augustine was oblivious of Him? Once again: Augustine cannot be *remembering* His presence as the basis of his recognition in the retelling.

His response to this enigma in the *Confessions* has two parts, First he has to formulate—in the tenth book—a theory of presence as an asymmetrical relation which may be converted to a symmetrical one. This is first done in spatial metaphor: he was outside himself, God was within; he was turned away, God was behind him, etc.; and then non-metaphorically in the language of presence, of "being-with" *mecum eras sed tecum non eram* (you were *with me*, but I was not *with you*). God is "most hidden and most present" (*secretissime et praesentissime*).[10]

But this step establishes only the *possibility* of recognizing God's having been with him, he all unknowing. What is the sufficient condition? It appears in the way in which Augustine was led to faith in the garden. We remarked that faith sees the history it narrates as having a second level of meaning exhibiting God's saving actions. In the *Confessions*, Augustine compares man's life to a sentence, whose sounds pass away, while the *sense* of the whole is collected in memory.[11] But just as sentences and texts have levels of meaning, so also for faith do human life and human history. It is in understanding the admonition *tolle, lege*, take and read, as "a command given to me by God" that Augustine comes slowly to realize that *all of the course of his life can be read* in that additional dimension. As was noted, this appears to be a constitutive element of the mode of belief we have called faith, namely that the additional level of meaning in events may in specific circumstances be understood as addressed uniquely to me.

It took Augustine a long time to arrive at this larger view. The *Confessions* was composed some ten to fifteen years after his conversion. The early philosophical dialogues, written while he was still in Milan, show no development of it. It is notable that in the *Confessions*, while he still speaks of God as the natural light of the soul, he does not identify that light with the Christ of history as he had done in the earlier dialogue *On the Teacher*. The historical dimension of faith opens a breach for him which prevents a too-easy identification of the God of philosophy with the God of Abraham, Isaac, and Jacob.

Even to speak of "history" is to risk a misunderstanding, for Augustine does not use the term in the *Confessions*, and his grasp of the meaning of his life's story is not that of a linear development. The meaning is based on a unified structure, namely of birth and descent, alienation from himself and from God, followed by ascent and rebirth, return to himself and the discovery of a new Father. His confidence in that insight leads him to try, in the last three books, to extend such an interpretation to the beginnings of the history of the world, a theme to which he returns years later in the *City of God*.

I have argued that the philosphical problematic which dominates *On the Teacher* is reprised and transcended in the *Confessions*. I want to consider briefly a second aspect of Augustine's belief in the latter work which might appear to be a residue of his earlier religious beliefs: his attitude toward the

preternatural. The *Confessions* records what he now perceives
as a credulousness. He believed in his Manichean years that
certain fruits contained bits of the divine substance, and that
those bits would be liberated from their material bondage if
one of the elect ate the fruit. Yet in the same period he abom-
inated the soothsayers, and though he consulted astrologers,
he constantly questioned himself and others about the credibility of their claims.

The Manichean beliefs he came to accept—though never,
as we have noted, wholly uncritically—apparently as an after-
math of being inspired, by the reading of Cicero, to seek wisdom. The Manichean teachings, like many in our own day,
offered a shortcut to that goal which filled the true believer
with a sense of the possession of esoteric wisdom and a superior-
ity over the uninitiated. The word 'God' was always on the lips
of his teachers, he says, but it was not God of whom they spoke.
Reference did not succeed because the sense was wrong.

Continuing to question and to test his beliefs, he came to
reject both Manicheanism and astrology, and returned to
philosophy in search of the credible.

Yet, as a Catholic Christian he accepted certain events as
evidently divine counsels, for example, the relief from a tooth-
ache as a response to prayers, the divine inspiration of Monica's
dreams (though he refers to his own dreams, he never interprets
them as religiously meaningful), a vision granted to Ambrose
as sent by God, and the miraculous healing of a blind man.

What shall we say of these things? That he has exchanged
one kind of credulousness for another? He was not, by tempera-
ment or training, a person attracted to the exotic or the occult.

In our day many do not consider it intellectually respectable
to believe such things as Augustine did. Yet the division between
the rational and the irrational is not the same as that between
the respectable and the suspect.

It is easy to lose one's footing here. Reason is in a no-man's
land, unmapped, not yet drawn into a conceptual framework
which fits into those frameworks familiar to us. Intellectual
comfort and the instinctive caution of reason resist the siren's
song, resist the stories about the *magnalia Dei* along with the

UFOs and ESP and Carlos Castaneda. But adamant skepticism is as irrational as pliant credulousness. Conceptual frameworks are extended, after all, not by logical inferences but by finding new data to be accounted for. We must "try the spirits whether they be of God"—or perhaps more apropos: (St. Paul) "do not be content to think childish thoughts; keep the innocence of children with the thought of grown men."

What prevents Augustine's acceptance of such preternatural events from being a return to a merely religious view is that he sees them as the unique responses of God to particular historical situations, as the gestural statements of One who stands over against us in alert concern. The Manichean teaching, in contrast, is of a struggle between good and evil whose basis lies before and beyond the creation of the world, of a divided will which is only the instantiation, the battlefield of that struggle, of an individual who has no permanent significance and hence for whom time is not crucial.

Turn to a final aspect of our book. It has been one of the most widely read books in every century since it was written. This implies obviously that very many people have read it for reasons other than the philosophical kind. They read it because it is, after all, a great story, well told.

Augustine himself says several times in the *Confessions* that there are two kinds of men, two kinds of readers. Speaking of the Scriptures, he says they are:

> easy for everyone to read and yet safeguarded the dignity of their hidden truth within a deeper meaning, by a lowly style of speech making itself accessible to all men, and drawing the attention of those who are not light of heart. Thus it can receive all men into its generous bosom, and by narrow passages lead on to You a small number of them.[12]

Later on he says:

> I myself—and I speak this fearlessly from my heart—if I were to write anything that would attain the highest level of authority, I would prefer to write in such manner that my words would sound forth the portion of truth each one man could take from those writings, rather than to put down one true opinion so obviously that it would exclude all others.[13]

We might reasonably suppose that the *Confessions* itself was written in this way, and that would justify not only the kind of exegesis we have done but encourage us to read the whole book with the care that Augustine applies to Genesis, in Books Eleven to Thirteen.

However that may be, we can safely say that philosophers and ordinary readers are likely to meet the text on different levels. Philosophers are disposed to "rationality"; they tend to state the meaning of a text in as clear and conceptually precise propositions as they can (or what seems to them clear and precise). That is, for them, the way toward and finally the embodiment of rationality.

But there is a fact staring us in the face here: *faith and religion tell stories to express their fundamental beliefs.* Not only can the categorial indicatives and imperatives in those stories not be excised from them and taken in isolation (as the Scripture scholars have been reminding us for a century or more), but the stories themselves embody meaning in a way which is not simply that of an *enchiridion symbolorum*, a set of propositions.

However important and even crucial it may be to formulate dogmatic and doctrinal clarifications which counter mistaken interpretations, it is the stories themselves which bear and retain the primary *and distinctive* level of meaning. It is the Christmas story and the Easter narrative and the parables to which the Christian believer turns—not to speculate on, but to meditate upon, in the effort to grasp the sense of the whole and of life.

Logos, we must not forget, can mean a story as well as reason and discourse. If we want to pose the question of the rationality of religion and faith, it cannot be on a Procrustean bed. We must ask not only whether it is rational to believe certain propositions; we must also ask *how* the *stories* (as stories) are "rational," or better, how they express and embody belief.

Augustine's *Confessions* is an account of his life, but an account which, in his meditation on and retelling of it, discloses a meaning of which he had not been aware in the living. Many have read it as a straightforward autobiography, just as Augustine says many read Scripture on that literal level.[14] We have pointed to a sequence of phases (religion, philosophy, faith) and to an underlying structure of meaning. But this amounts to little more than pointing out that the work has a greater complexity than first appears; it is like saying that the *Odyssey* is the story of a homecoming. For it is the narrative structure and its profusion of biblical images through which Augustine understands what happened to him that bear and flesh out, give substance to, the underlying structure. And it is that narrative and those images which have engaged generations of thoughtful readers and quickened the spirit of their understanding.

It is not illegitimate for philosophers to discuss the rationality of faith or of a story in terms of the rationality of believing a proposition; but the former is not reducible to the latter. The *logos* (story) of Exodus has still to be properly related to the *logoi* of the philosophers.

NOTES

1. For some relevant discussion from the extensive literature on oral tradition, cf. W. Ong, S. J., *Presence of the Word* (New Haven, Conn., 1967) and *Interfaces of the Word* (Ithaca, N.Y., 1977); E. Havelock, *Preface to Plato* (Cambridge, Mass., 1963).

2. *Confessions* V, 3:6. All references are to the *Confessions* unless otherwise noted.

3. I, 8. I pass over the question of whether Augustine's theory of language learning is justly criticized by Wittgenstein in *Philosophical Investigations* I, #32. He understands Augustine to assume that learning a first language is essentially the same as learning a second language, hence implicitly supposing that the problem of meaning is already solved. But it would appear that Augustine's theory is more adequately understood by relating it to Husserl's notion of a prepredicative level of meaning which is different in kind from the meaning of words but still related as a kind of meaning. Certainly Augustine did not have the simple "Fido—'Fido'" theory which some of Wittgenstein's epigones have foisted on him: e.g., the saint's discussion of 'nihil' in the *de Magistro*, II.

4. VII, 17; X, 10, 12.

5. X, 18, 19. The similarity of the problematic here to that of Kierkegaard in the *Philosophical Fragments* is manifest. In my view, this work can be read as a commentary on the *Confessions*.

6. Compare *De Vera Religione* XXXVI, 66: *veritas est qua ostenditur id quod est.*

7. III, 12; IX, 8:17. These passages are sometimes cited to support the contention that there is no formal structure. It is "a badly composed book"; it is "a commonplace of Augustinian scholarship to say that Augustine was not able to plan a book": John J. O'Meara, *The Young Augustine* (New York, 1965), pp. 13, 44. A summary of various attempts to find such a unifying interpretation is in P. Courcelles, *Recherches sur les Confessions de saint Augustin* (Paris, 1950), pp. 21 ff. For a recent discussion and summary (and another attempt) see Robert J. O'Connell, *St. Augustine's Confessions: The Odyssey of a Soul* (Cambridge, Mass., 1969), pp. 3-22.

8. *Retractiones* 32.

9. IX, 12:29.

10. X, 27; I, 4. God's "unilateral" omnipresence is, of course, precisely the problem proposed in the opening of Book One.

11. XI, 28; IV, 11.

12. VI, 5.

13. XII, 31.

14. A recent and competent translator, for example, comments that Augustine is "naturally concerned" in Book Ten with the character and operation of memory "because he has completed the prodigious feat of memory that finds expression in Books 1-9."